LA GOMERA FOR V

GW00733357

Lance Chilton

Published in 2000 by MARENGO PUBLICATIONS
17 Bernard Crescent, Hunstanton PE36 6ER
United Kingdom.

Printed by Catford Print Centre
3 Bellingham Road, London SE6 4PY.

Text and maps © copyright 2000, Lance Chilton.

All rights reserved. No part of this publication may be reproduced in any form without permission from the publisher except for the quotation of brief passages in reviews.

ISBN 1 900802 67 8

Unless described otherwise, all these walk routes are in reasonable condition, but this situation can change quickly in an area of sometimes violent weather and subsequent land-slips or altered surfaces - not to mention the effect of bulldozers. Most paths have at least some loose stones, and rain can very quickly make the steeper ones unsuitable for the less agile, or indeed for anyone. Written for the active walker, none of the walks are intended as a light stroll or are suitable for someone with, for example, dodgy ankles, bad knees or a serious weight or health problem.

The **weather** on Gomera can be very variable, particularly in the upper areas, where extremely cold fog can appear out of warm sunshine in a few minutes. You should be prepared for hot sun and cold rain! Spare warm clothes **and** waterproofs are essential in the higher areas, and recommended for the lower ones. Think carefully before attempting high walks in wet or misty weather - not only may the climatic conditions be unpleasant, but high bus stops for your return have little or no shelter. Rain can be very heavy when it does occur and can make paths treacherous, or even impassable. It frequently causes small and large rockfalls, both on roads and paths. Where the following walks include sections on main roads, which do not have pavements, these should only be undertaken in weather conditions with reasonable visibility for the approaching traffic.

In the text, **views** of the island and of Tenerife, Hierro and La Palma are mentioned - these views are of course dependent on clear weather! On occasions you can see Gran Canaria clearly, on others you may see little more than a couple of metres in front of you. After long periods of dry weather, streams, waterfalls or lakes mentioned in the text may be nonexistent.

Anyone using this book does so at their own risk. Although the author has used all the routes described without any mishap, and has tried to describe the routes as accurately as possible, he cannot accept any responsibility for incidents occurring during the use of this book. Please read through the *entire* description of a walk before attempting it.

Route times at the beginning of a walk description are *approximate* times for *faster* walkers on *dry* paths and do not allow for rest-stops, miradors, picnics, photography and so on. It is particularly difficult to give meaningful times for Gomera's steep ascents and descents, since there will be much variation in pace from person to person. If you are slower, do not attempt to hurry, but enjoy the walk at your own pace. The length of a description does not necessarily relate to the length of the walk. A walk can be long and complicated or short and involved. Not all the paths are well-surfaced. Some of the routes described need care and reasonable agility.

Compass directions in the text are approximate and a compass is not necessary for any of the walks.

Altitudes of locations are given in brackets. Heights of peaks are the summit height, not those of your path if near the peak. Villages on slopes can have a considerable altitude gain from one end of the village to the other - some 300m at Taguluche, for instance.

A '**track**' in the text is a vehicle-width dirt-track - though not necessarily driveable! Some tracks in the National Park have a chained barrier, to stop vehicles but not pedestrians. Elsewhere on the island, chains often indicate a private road with no pedestrian access. **Privado** means private.

- A **barranco** is a steep sided valley.
- An **ermita** is a small, usually isolated, church or chapel.
- A **fortaleza** is a flat plateau produced by the accumulation of thick and pasty lava outside a volcanic chimney.
- A **mirador** is a place with a view. Some are manmade, while others are just natural lookout points.
- **Power-towers** are the Gomeran equivalents of a pylon - a square, concrete, tower building supporting electricity cables and fittings. Metal pylons also occur.
- A **roque** is a pointed outcrop of acidic rock, formed by the lava cooling inside a volcanic chimney, and exposed through erosion of material outside the chimney. There are a number of examples on Gomera, particularly around Roque Agando.

Mention of bars, cafés, restaurants, hotels and shops by name is for directional purposes only and should not be taken as the author's endorsement or recommendation. Note that small shops and bars often do not have a name-sign, and may just appear to be house doorways if they are closed.

Unlike much of the Mediterranean, Gomera does not have an abundance of spiny native plants. However, a couple of introduced plants can cause damage. Prickly pear cacti are fairly obvious, but the large succulent rosettes of Agave are more dangerous, with their sharply pointed and tooth-edged bluish-grey leaves, which can easily draw blood if you brush against them incautiously.

In 1996-97 many signs in the Garajonay park were replaced by more detailed signs giving distances to various points. However, please note that the distances given on signs at successive junctions do not always calculate correctly, with errors of up to 0.4km in some cases.

Not all the walks can be made using public transport to reach start and end points, however the following can (with a short connecting walk to or from the bus-stop in some cases): Walks 1, 2, 7, 12, 13, 15, 20, 23, 26, 27*, 29, 34*, 36, 37, 39* and 40* (*=assuming an appropriate Line-2 bus via Alajeró). The following are circular, with the start point on a bus route: 4, 5, 6, 16, 17, 19, 22 and 25.

Gomeran Spanish is perhaps easier for English speakers to pronounce than much mainland Spanish, however remember that:

Spanish V is like an English B
Spanish J is like the CH in Scottish *loch*
Spanish H is silent
Gomeran LL is pronounced something between Y and the LLI in *million*
Vowels with an accent should be stressed.

1 Hermigua to Riscos de Juel to Casas de Enchereda to Carretera del Norte

Hermigua is a village consisting of a long 5km of clustered settlements along the Barranco de Monteforte. There is over 300m altitude gain from the seaward end (*Playa*) to the top, so it is worth ensuring the bus stops at the right place. Allow 2.5 hours to Riscos de Juel, and another 2.5 hours to the Carretera del Norte.

Ask for **Playa de Hermigua** and the bus will drop you at a junction, by a phone kiosk, where the asphalt road to Playa drops down towards the sea. Follow this road to the *Faro* bar/restaurant. Turn right immediately before the bar and go down steps to pass the *Playa Apartments*. The way narrows and finally a few steps down bring you out onto the asphalt road. Turn right. After crossing a bridge, the road divides - left to the old jetty site and right into the Altonazo area. Between the roads, a signpost to *La Caleta* marks steps with green railings. Go up the first flight of concrete steps then, before the second, turn left immediately after a very low concrete wall. It looks like a stream bed to start with, but it is the path. It zigzags up past the first few houses, then out onto the left-hand side of a deep gully. Stay with the path on the left, taking upward options at forks in the path. Pass between a final house and its large palm tree, walking under the house's vine frame. The path zigzags up to the ridge where it meets a dirt track at a 3-way junction, with a broken signpost.

Look over the ridge. From here there are two possible routes for the next section of the main walk. The first is described immediately below, and the second one, via La Caleta, is described at the end of the main walk details. See ■. A third, much shorter, walk to La Caleta beach and back is also possible. See ●.

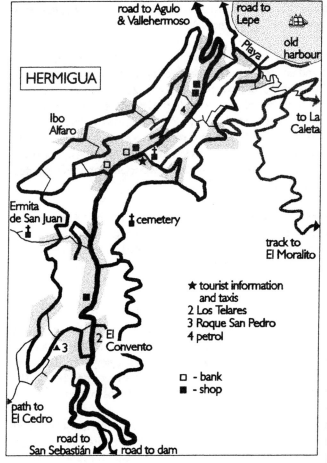

HERMIGUA

road to Agulo & Vallehermoso

road to Lepe

old harbour

Playa

Ibo Alfaro

to La Caleta

Ermita de San Juan

cemetery

track to El Moralito

★ tourist information and taxis
2 Los Telares
3 Roque San Pedro
4 petrol

□ - bank
■ - shop

2 El Convento

▲ 3

path to El Cedro

road to San Sebastián

road to dam

From the 3-way junction on the ridge above Playa de Hermigua, go uphill and to the right, inland. Follow the track along the contours of the hillside, through many winding curves. Ignore a left turn down to a couple of houses in a deep valley below. At a junction just beyond a little white shrine set into the right bank, stay left on the main track where the upper track is (sometimes) chained off. Your track goes above a little water channel that bridges a stream. Beyond the stream is a low stone house among palm trees.

A couple of abandoned houses, and more houses just above on the hillside and in front of you, is the hamlet of **El Moralito**. The track turns through a luxuriant streambed, with pines and junipers. Large areas of the Juel ridge, which this walk takes you up to, come into view round a corner, but ignore a track up to the right. At a sharp turn through a wooded gully, ignore a track that goes down to the left.

Ignore the next, chained-off, right turn, at a ridge. Take the following right turn, after a long low line of buildings, partly orange-tiled, comes into view on the left of the track.

The main track goes onwards, left, to Agen del Palmar and Tagaluche. *The alternative route, via La Caleta, comes in here* (see below•).

Your upward track passes some large palms and rounds a dark-soil corner with dripping water, then zigzags up and up. You appear to be reaching the top at an apparent col, by the Roque Caraballo (576m/1890ft), but there is another 200m of ascent remaining up the **Riscos de Juel**. Pass a couple of tiny houses to the left of the road, one of them with a solar panel. You may have spotted these much earlier, from below. The track continues to zigzag up, sliced deeply through the rock in places and with vertical cliffs above you on the left-hand side. After final spectacular views northwest, north and northeast, you are enclosed in cooler pine and laurel woodland for a few minutes. Climb to a makeshift wooden gate.

Emerge past a locked well and a lamp standard, into a more open area of tree heather vegetation. After a couple of descending loops the track swings southwest into the Barranco de Juel valley. This end of the valley is open, with black rocks on the right, but further in there is pine woodland. After entering the depths of the valley, the track turns and climbs, with laurel and heather woodland on the right.

The track rises to another ridge, swings around a corner and reveals views right across to the radio mast on Tagamiche (979m/3210ft), several ridges away to the south. The next valley is that of the Barranco de Galión. On the inward stretch there is a metal gate. Please close this after you, to stop the local cows from straying. After this valley, there are a few false corners before you are round into the Barranco de Majona. This valley is the largest of the three and the one with the most loops in the track.

The track makes a long loop into the valley head's first gully. *The old, now-closed path over Mt Enchereda (1065m/3495ft) goes off to the right, from a later gully.* Pass the buildings of **Casas de Enchereda** (590m/1935ft), probably with the smell of wood smoke in the air. Cheese is made here and young goats wander around the buildings.

The path up and over the ridge between you and the Carretera del Norte should be clearly visible running diagonally across the hillside ahead. The beginning of this path is some way beyond the Casas, and starts as wide steps. It climbs to over 700m and then drops a couple of hundred to the Carretera del Norte. Alternatively, stay with the track which runs at least another 1.25km along the north side of the ridge to a pass at 600m. *From the pass, an onward path goes, via Mt Jaragán (612m/2005ft), down to the upper part of San Sebastián* (**Walk 2**). Your route, the *Forestal de Majona* track, swings back around the south side of the ridge. There are tremendous views of San Sebastián to the southeast and of the Carretera del Norte immediately below. The track winds down to join the Carretera, at the same point on the San Sebastián-Hermigua-Vallehermoso bus route as the path over the top.

●Playa de la Caleta Walk

The left and downhill track seen in the valley ahead of you winds down to the beach at La Caleta. Look to the right of this track, just below, for a wall-like sill of rock that slopes down towards a lower part of the beach track. The path goes down to the left of and alongside the sill, then swings across to the right. It is fractured lower down, but follow the best options, and cut off a long loop of the track. Turn right at the bottom, onto the track, by a dry streambed.

At a later corner where the track swings right and ruined houses and terraces come into view, there is a possible path off ahead along a small ridge. However, this path is deteriorating, and there is a metre or so drop at the end to get back onto the track. If you stay with the track, this leads down to the final steps to the beach. Resist the little wooden suspension bridge on your right, which goes only to a house and terraces. The beach is larger than early glimpses suggested, with the Ermita of San Juan, several fishing boats, loos, and some refreshment stalls (closed in winter). There is black sand on part of the beach, rocks on the rest. The view of Tenerife and Mt Teide can be spectacular. Return by the same route.

■Playa de Hermigua to La Caleta to Agen del Palmar, then either on to Riscos de Juel to Casas de Enchereda to Carretera del Norte or back to Playa de Hermigua

The Agen del Palmar route is an alternative to part of the main walk, probably shorter and quicker, more varied, but more vertiginous. Follow the main route to the 3-way junction on the first ridge. The left and downhill track in the valley ahead of you winds down to the beach at La Caleta. Look to the right of this track, just below, for a wall-like sill of rock that slopes down towards a lower part of the beach track. The path goes down to the left of and alongside the sill, then swings across to the right. It is fractured lower down, but follow the best options, and cut off a long loop of the track. Turn right at the bottom onto the track, by a dry streambed.

At a later corner the track swings right and ruined houses and terraces come into view. Just past the next left-hand curve of the track, join a small path going down right to the stream. Cross the streambed and start to climb between terraces, but, after a minute, turn off left onto a path edged by spiky *Agave* plants. This path swings around the hillside, rising high above La Caleta beach and beyond. In places, sections of the path have been partly washed away, and though still passable at the time of writing, can be narrow. Where the path forks clearly, go right, uphill. The vertiginous section ends by the stream bed of a small, palmy valley, where the path splits again. Go back left (not straight on) across the stream and then up the hillside. At the next ridge, follow a channel in the rock up to the right.

Stay with the path, which is faint in places, up the hillside until you reach one of the few houses of Agen del Palmar. Surprisingly, this is not the large house that first became visible above as you climbed. Go immediately to the right of the house and along the back to join a rough and disintegrating dirt track. Follow this to a parking area on a ridge, and turn back right onto a higher track. The other track, onward left from the ridge, leads, though it is no longer driveable, towards Tagaluche. Your track goes back past the other houses of Agen del Palmar, and an amazing vineyard built in an avalanche of huge boulders. Look out for a long, low line of buildings, partly orange-tiled, on the right. Beyond these, a track marked by two small posts leads back up the hillside and is your onward route if you join the main walk*. Alternatively you can stay with the main track back to Playa de Hermigua in about two hours.

2 Carretera del Norte to Jaragán to San Sebastian

This walk starts from the San Sebastián-Hermigua road, the Carretera del Norte, about 8.5km out of San Sebastián, at the junction of the road and the forestal (dirt road) to Enchereda. It could be combined with **Walk I**, from Hermigua to the Carretera del Norte, to make one (very) long walk.

From the junction on the **Carretera del Norte**, start up the forestal road, but moments after leaving the asphalt road go left onto a path. Follow the zigzags of this path up the hillside and in about 25 minutes reach the top of the narrow ridge, and a view beyond into the Barranco de Majona. A path goes off left, towards the buildings of the Enchereda cheese factory. This path rejoins the dirt road in about 15 minutes, which then leads eventually to lower Hermigua. However, your route is the narrow path to the *right* from the col, which remains on the southern, Carretera side of the ridge. Wind-shaped trees indicate the prevailing weather just here. The path is slightly vertiginous in places, but the ridge soon broadens out and the path takes you down towards the Forestal road, which has made a large circle in front. Jaragán peak is ahead of you. Cairns mark the descent to the dirt road.

Join the road in just over half an hour's walk from the Carretera. At the point where the road swings around the corner to the right and across the ridge, look to the left-hand side of the eastward ridge. Paint marks indicate the start of the path. Initially this is to the left of the ridge, but it soon climbs up and swings over to the Carretera side, where mostly it stays. After about 12 minutes from the dirt road, a distinct, rubbish-strewn path goes steeply up the cliff to the right. Look up and you will see the television aerial of the **Jaragán** house. This path goes to the house and also to the start of the Cuevas Blancas path, however the house and surroundings are patrolled by free-range guard dogs, so it is suggested that you take a large stick. There is an alternative route to Cuevas Blancas from further along your cliff-path ■, but please read the following before you decide.

> **Cuevas Blancas**. Some reference sources suggest this detour for seeing interesting rock formations. However, 40 minutes' walk will just bring you to an isolated breeze-block hovel, with more, unfriendly dogs. The route starts from the top of the ridge behind the Jaragán house, but it can also be reached from further along **Walk 2**, where indicated, to avoid going so near to the house.

Continue along the mostly level cliff path to the *end* of the cliffs.

> ■ At this point it is easy to go back up to the left onto the open ridge, and north-northwest for Cuevas Blancas, along the seaward side of the ridge. The main path swings right and down to some ruined houses, just before the spine of the Cuevas Blancas ridge, but various goat-paths lead diagonally right earlier to reach the same houses. From the ruins, paths lead you out to the right of a further ruin, and along the ridge, the Lomo de Majona. Return is by the same route.

However, the main walk continues on southeastward from the end of the cliffs, in the direction of San Sebastián. A thin path goes on ahead to the point of the ridge, but look out for a cairned path leading off to the left. This zigzags diagonally down the hillside, then heads back right to circle around the back of a large rocky bowl, the top of the Barranco de Avalo. Emerge from the bowl about 20 minutes later, and follow a clear path down the ridge. The route is straightforward from here. About 2 hours from the start of the walk, join a dirt track and go right. Follow this track down towards **San Sebastián**, passing a radio mast and hut on right.

Join an asphalt road, and go downhill into the upper suburbs of the capital. Several streets come in from the left, but after passing a street going sharply back left, then another above left, look to the right for the side street *Nunez de Balbo*. This is by a yellow postbox. Take the steps here, going down then left. Go left and down, then right and down, to pass a looping corner of the descending road. From this corner go down steps. At the next section of road, go along to the right, then take the steps down beside a telephone kiosk. Continue down on pink tiles and turn left at the next junction. At a 3-way junction, moments later, take the middle option, to emerge behind the church of Nostra Señora de la Asunción. Join the road Calle Real (del Medio), and turn left for the centre of town.

3 Hermigua to Roque San Pedro to El Cedro to Alto de Contadero

Allow about 3-4 hours to Alto de Contadero. From Alto de Contadero you can go on to Pajarito or Las Paredes to meet the buses on the Santiago-San Sebastián (not all services) or Valle Gran Rey-San Sebastián routes. This walks starts from the **El Convento** (220m/720ft) area of upper Hermigua. The bus stops by the high white walls of the Los Telares shop and small museum. Look to the left, if you are facing seaward, for a double set of steps leading up from near the corner of the road just below Los Telares, and take the left-hand flight. This brings you up to the higher asphalt road. Turn right. Building # 51 is a gofio mill and you may smell the ground maize as you pass. *Gofio* is used as an optional thickener at the table for some soups. Not many restaurants seem now to offer it to tourists but, if you do have it, try it sparingly at first as the taste can be strong. Continue along, around a corner of the asphalt. Roque San Pedro and its smaller companion loom over the road on your left, and shortly after you should turn left off the asphalt and cross a footbridge.

Over the footbridge, go right along the left-hand side of the stream. Where good steps go up left, stay instead with the stream, following the rocky bed in places through the reeds. After several minutes you cross a little stone and concrete footbridge to a path, marked by blue paint, off right between high terrace walls. The path and steps lead up to a large, dark-green water pipe, with a yellow **H** on the left wall just before it. *This H is the only marker here if you are doing the route in reverse. Alternatively, coming down, you can stay with the path by the water pipe and join the upper asphalt road on the western side of the valley.* Turn left and follow the green pipe upvalley, until you reach a water tank at a gorge-like narrowing of the valley. Your path leads up left, sometimes on rocky steps, behind the tank, then climbs to the right. Continue upvalley with this path. When you reach the large dam, cross a footbridge just before it, to the right, and climb the *stone* steps.

There are concrete steps up on the left, but these lead to a dirt track accessing the dam from the road above Hermigua. It is not possible to cross from this dirt track directly to the El Cedro path if the dam lake is full.

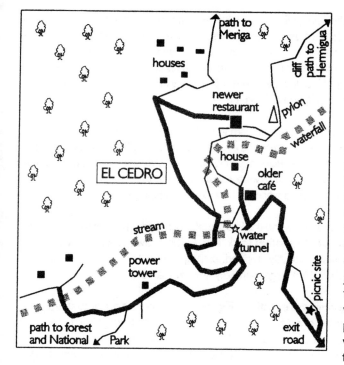

At the top of the stone steps, the path leads alongside the right of the dam lake. It then starts the main climb to El Cedro, to the right of a huge part-circle of cliffs. An immensely tall, but usually thin, waterfall comes into view. The path will climb to cross the skyline just to the right of the top of this waterfall, by the pylon. The forest is visible along the top of the surrounding cliffs.

Follow the path, which zigzags up the cliff face, passing several outlying laurel species. For the botanically minded, this is a good site for the laurel *Apollonias*, usually recognizable by the characteristic mite-induced blisters that scar its leaves. The path is mostly of a reasonable width, though occasionally narrow, steep, and a little vertiginous. There are some spectacular views, looking back over the Hermigua valley.

Shortly after the pylon, the path nears the waterfall stream and then swings into the much softer scenery of the hanging valley of **El Cedro** (850m/2790ft). *Be aware that El Cedro is very prone to misty or foggy conditions, which can come in very suddenly, cutting off all views of the valley. When this happens, it usually also affects at least the first, lower part of the onward route to Alto de Contadero.* Up on the right, a little signed path leads to a small campsite and a restaurant. The main path runs alongside the stream, then crosses it and runs up beside a fenced house. The large dogs here are noisy and may leap aggressively against the fence as you pass. There is an alternate path across the stream, to the right at the bottom of the paved slope. Just above the house is an older café - not always open.

A dirt track up from the older café, concrete-surfaced in places, is the 2.7km exit road for the hamlet. It climbs to the main Carretera Dorsal/Carretera de Rejo asphalt road 250m higher. About 700m along this track, a short entrance road back up to the left goes to a flat area, with some roofed picnic tables. Around the tables are planted several interesting local shrubs, including the pale blue flowered Echium acanthocarpum, and Euphorbia lambii, both rare and only found on Gomera.

Across the track from the café, a little path goes down to a small tunnel mouth, and a footbridge over the stream. This tunnel is a water channel through the ridge southeast of the village, to the Carretera de Rejo. It is possible to walk through if you have a torch, however, the heavy rains of the 95/96 winter washed away part of the exit path at the far end putting it out of action for a while and this could happen again.

Cross the footbridge and follow the track to the left, as it winds uphill for a few minutes, then take the right turn onto another track. Pass a white power-tower on your right. Beyond it there is a first, distinctly stepped, path up on the left, but take the second upward, wider, earth path. A large painted yellow **H** marks it.

Follow the path, ignoring smaller paths going down to the right. You climb steeply into an open area, then to a view of some houses. Follow the path through the hamlet and after passing the very last of the houses, the main path swings left suddenly into the sunless depths of the laurel forest. This is the start of the **Garajonay National Park**.

If the sun was out in El Cedro, then the forest will be cooler. If the sun was not out, then the forest will probably be cold. The dense laurel tree branches above efficiently cut out much of the light, and if you try to take a photograph you will discover just how low the light levels are. The stream is in the depths below you to the right. Lush ferns colonize all the slopes around.

This is part of the Canary Islands' largest surviving area of **laurisilva**, the ancient evergreen laurel forest that once covered the Mediterranean and western Canaries. Laurisilva had died out in the Mediterranean 15 million years ago, due to ice ages and desertification, but survived in the Canaries until recent times. Human activities such as timber cutting, charcoal production, agriculture and the use of groundwater, have devastated the laurisilva on the other Canary Islands. An area of 4000 hectares (15.4 square miles) on Gomera was declared the Garajonay National Park in 1981, and in 1986 it became a UNESCO World Heritage site. Paths and routes within the park are restricted to certain areas, and much of it left more or less inaccessible in order to preserve it. More details can be found at the excellent Visitors' Centre (**Walks 3 & 4**).

Walk on, to pass the locked-up Ermita de Nostre Señora de Lourdes and its picnic site, and cross the little footbridge to reach the right-hand side of the stream. Your path then climbs, and the way is clear as it follows the line of the stream to join a dirt track at **Las Mimbreras**. The *Rejo Pista Forestal* track comes in from the left. Go right with the track to cross the stream. Your path off left is chained, and signed *3A Las Mimbreras to Alto de Contadero*. You may find the two hours suggested by the sign for the route is nearer 50-75 minutes.

The dirt track further right passes small excavations in the bank and goes, eventually, to the hamlets of Los Aceviños and Meriga, as detailed at the end of this walk.

Just before the next junction, the distinctive, huge-leaved *Woodwardia* or chain fern is visible on the far bank of the stream, through the trees to your left. This plant only survives in the dampest parts of the forest.

You come to a crossroads of paths. The main path goes on and upwards. A second, older path goes off back down to the right. Go left on a third path. This bridges the stream, wanders along beside or above it, recrosses by rough stepping stones, and then climbs to rejoin the main path where you turn left. The main path then takes you under a tunnel of tall broom bushes leading to an open area. A large sign points to *Alto de Contadero* and *Garajonay*. Ignore a path back off to the right.

Pass a sign marked *Campamento Antiguo* and soon you are among tall, fine-leaved tree heathers. A once very large sweet-chestnut tree - now partly collapsed - is to the right of the path. An ascent of 350m follows. Stay with the long winding path as it climbs to the car-park at **Alto de Contadero** (1350m/4430ft).

You can arrange in advance for a taxi pickup here - tell them Contadero, at the top of the El Cedro path. The nearest bus stop is at Pajarito, several kilometres along the winding asphalt road to the left, or over the top via or past Garajonay summit. *From Contadero it is possible to continue, with **Walk 22**, to Chipude.*

Alto de Contadero to Garajonay

From Contadero, you can go on to Garajonay summits in about 25 minutes, part of **Walk 20** in reverse. To do so, leave the car-park by the left entrance, cross the asphalt road, and head up the signed track. Join a footpath to the left, signed to the summit. This climbs the ridge and then swings to the right, crossing a small dip in the ridge before finally rising to the summit.

Alternatively, stay with the track (not joining the footpath) and at a signposted junction of tracks, turn left to the summit. In bad weather the section from Contadero to Garajonay is very exposed and liable to have no views at all.

Alto de Contadero to Las Paredes or Pajarito

Cross the road and head uphill. Stay with the main track until a signposted junction of dirt tracks where left is to Alto de Garajonay (the summit). Go with the chained track to the right but then go left at the next junction shortly afterwards. Follow the dirt track around to the south side of Garajonay, until a clear fork in the track - onward left goes to Pajarito and onward right to Las Paredes. With the latter route, on reaching the asphalt, head left and downhill to the junction just below, where you can catch the Santiago (not all services) or Valle Gran Rey buses.

Alternatively go left at that first signposted junction of dirt tracks, but look for a path leading up the bank to the left by the junction. This leads to a cross paths - right goes to Garajonay summit, but go straight across and you join a wider dirt track which leads down to towards Las Paredes (see map). **Walk 26** continues via Igualero to Fortaleza (and Chipude).

Las Mimbreras to El Cedro I (West)

From Las Mimbreras it is possible to follow the Los Aceviños/Meriga track, which gradually climbs the western side of the El Cedro valley. Almost at the top of the track, just before a left curve and a junction with another track, two green spots high on the left-hand rock wall mark a path down to the right. This steep little path through the laurels leads to another path, which goes off to the right to El Cedro. It emerges from the forest near scattered houses on the western valley slope above the newer restaurant. Descend past the lower houses to the end of a dirt track which leads left to the restaurant or down and right to the valley stream by the footbridge and water tunnel mentioned earlier.

Las Mimbreras to El Cedro 2 (East)

From Las Mimbreras take the *Rejo Pista Forestal* track which gradually climbs the southeastern side of the El Cedro valley. At a 3-way track junction, left leads you back down to El Cedro, passing the picnic table area mentioned in the main walk.

Las Mimbreras to Los Aceviños to Meriga to the Visitors' Centre

From the green dots, in the **Las Mimbreras-El Cedro I** paragraph, it is possible to stay on the dirt track to Los Aceviños and Meriga. This is an attractive route with a lot of more open laurel forest en route, but it is a long way - further than it looks from most maps. Once you get to Meriga there is asphalt on to the Visitors' Centre, and beyond. Continue past the green dots. Swing left and then continue left when a track joins yours from the right. Stay with the main track as it follows the contour of the hills, gradually descending. At the next and following ridge corners, ignore tracks off right. Descend with the track to the west side of the cultivated **Los Aceviños** valley and a signed junction, where you turn left - as opposed to right for Los Aceviños. This onward track climbs the long western flank of the Los Aceviños valley, rounds into an upper branch of the Meriga valley, then gradually descends through wild avocado forest to a parking space.

Here it joins the end of the **Meriga** asphalt road. Several interesting endemic Canarian and Gomeran shrubs are planted here, and there is a nearby nursery for young laurels (not for sale!). The shrubs include *Arbutus canariensis*, *Echium acanthocarpum*, *Euphorbia lambii*, *E. mellifera*, *Heberdenia excelsa*, *Juniperus cedrus*, *Maytenus canariensis*, *Pericallis hansenii*, *Rhamnus glandulosa* and *Sambucus palmensis*. An information sign suggests you should get to know which is which, but unfortunately the individual shrubs are not labelled. The level

asphalt road leads to La Palmita, and then, eventually, to the Visitors' Centre.

Meriga to the Visitor's Centre

Another asphalt road goes steeply up left, from the parking space by the Meriga laurel nursery. It leads up to the Laguna Grande-Visitors' Centre road. Go right for the Visitors' Centre, but watch out for large tourist coaches.

4 Agulo to the Visitors' Centre to La Palmita to Agulo

Important! Usually the Visitors' Centre is closed only on Mondays, but sometimes in winter it also closes on Sundays. If you are planning to call in, then check opening times, *before* you go, perhaps at the tourist information offices in central Hermigua, Santiago or San Sebastián. Allow about 4 hours for the walk, plus plenty of time at the Centre.

Agulo village (200m/655ft) perches on a shelf overlooking the sea and Tenerife, and is almost completely cut off from the rest of Gomera by a semicircle of 300m high cliffs. Care has been taken to retain the old character of the village, which is in three parts and one of the most attractive on the island.

From the Agulo bus stop on the main road, looking in the Vallehermoso direction, turn right into Agulo village just before the *Casa Aixa* shop, where the road on towards

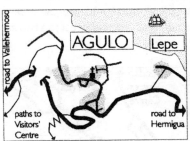

Vallehermoso swings left. Turn right at the *Alameda* bar and shop. The *Caja Canarias* bank is on the right of the road through this part of the village. Leave the houses and follow the cobbles across into the central part of the village, going left at the road junction between the two parts. From the main square of the central part go up to the left of the unusual, dark grey and white, domed church, on the street called *Calle de Pedro Bethancourt*.

Follow this street through the central part of the village and then down through a lower part to the white horseshoe-shaped cemetery of Agulo, which is marked by a large dark oriental *Ficus* tree. Beyond the cemetery your path goes steeply up to the left, where the new concrete road continues on the level. Your path rises to a landslide area where it is partly disrupted and perhaps likely to disappear completely in due course, and on to a narrow col. A water pipe comes in from the left just before the col. Follow the path beside this pipe up to the main Agulo-Vallehermoso road beyond the Agulo tunnel.

Alternatively, from the cemetery, follow the concrete road around the end of the ridge, then take zigzag paths up to the main asphalt road.

Turn right onto the asphalt, with the tunnel mouth on your left. After a short distance, a green arrow marks the obvious start of your path up from the inland side of the road.

The path zigzags and climbs. It is quite clear at first, but later is not as wide and is somewhat overgrown in places. Occasionally it may be easier to walk on the wall alongside the path. Pass a big curve of cliffs with a red rock waterfall, followed by a second big curve. The path is overgrown here. The scattered houses of Las Rosas village and the top of the valley come into view. You seem to be getting near the top of the ridge, but this is merely illusory. At what appears to be a T-junction, take the left turn, and climb with the path by a series of zigzags. Your path then winds across to the right, and tree heather scrub comes into view higher up on your left.

The path approaches some red earth cliffs and then turns left. There is a short section here where the path is really overgrown and you must scramble over or beside an orange rock outcrop to the left of the path. This can be a little tricky if it is very windy.

Here there are views out to the right, to the edge of Las Rosas. Nearby there is a long low building built into the hillside and, above it, large pine trees. The path swings right to go above and behind the building. Just behind it, before the first pine tree, your path branches off up to the left. This path zigzags upwards, passing a few outlying laurels. As you near some pine trees, the original cobbled and paved path appears, but it soon merges into the surface of the rock in a more open area.

A bare water-gully runs diagonally off to the right and cairns point you, apparently, to a path through the heather. Stay near to the left-hand side of the gully, in this area of bright red clay. Join a vehicle-width track marked by stones, and that can be seen running off along the side of the ridge to the right. By a small clump of pines, it merges

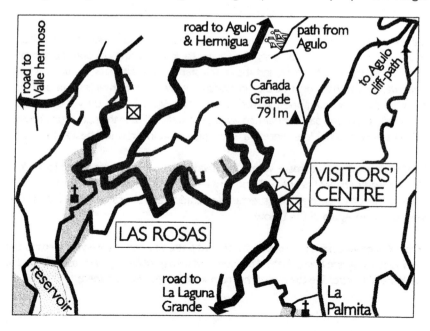

with another track, coming in from the left. Continue straight on. Pass a couple of small buildings and drop down to the asphalt road that has been visible for a while. Go right, with the valley on your left.

Round a corner and the **Visitors' Centre**, *Juego de Bolas*, (750m/2460ft) comes into view on your right, with the *Tambor* bar/restaurant ahead. Both are closed on Mondays. When the Centre is open it is well worth a visit. There are informative displays on the geology, ecology and vegetation, books for sale, and a film show about the islands is available on request. In separate buildings there are toilets and craft shops, and a small ethnic museum with slides and music (de Falla: *Cadiz*). The garden has a good selection of Canarian and Gomeran endemics and some of the laurels. If you are interested in the plants, this is a good place to start learning to recognize some of them when seen growing wild later during your stay. There are further plants in pots in the main building's inner courtyard, including the rare and spectacular, orange-flowered, climbing Canary bellflower, *Canarina*, and a collection of the succulent endemic *Aeonium* species. Entrance is free.

Continue past the Visitors' Centre, on the asphalt road along the ridge, and take the turning on the left down to **La Palmita** village (690m/2265ft). The road through the village reaches a little promontory with a church and buildings on it. Take the paved ramp down from this, on the right-hand side beyond the church.

Just above a concrete platform, turn left at a T-junction. Join a dirt track and turn left and down. Follow this dirt track along the valley, back below and beyond the Visitors' Centre. Just after a wet corner, and above a cluster of houses, the track splits. Take the downward track on the right. At the junction just below, go left towards a dam and lake. Near this dam there is a stone and wood signpost for *Agulo*. Follow the walled path, up to the left, above and past the dam, to where the wall ends and the path zigzags down to join another path. Here there is a water pipe sunk in a channel beside the path.

Further down there is damage where floodwater has come in from a gully to the left. Cross a water channel near a wall and turn left to an obvious path/streambed which leads, a little off to the right, to a spectacular mirador, and an astonishingly vertiginous view down to Agulo 300m below.

If you change your mind here about the onward path, you can retrace your steps to the track junction by the houses behind the dam and then go uphill to join an asphalt road to the Visitors' Centre. See the end of the main walk for options from there.

At the Agulo mirador the path goes off to the left and works its way down the cliff-face. The engineering of the path is remarkable here and the views can be distracting. Please stop walking if you want to look around or out and down, otherwise concentrate on the path. Eventually you will have descended to a less vertical section of hillside, and can follow steps down between cultivated terraces to the asphalt road.

Go straight across the road and follow the water pipe that turns right below a wall. Just past a creeper-covered wall on the left, the pipe divides. Go with the left fork to arrive back at a lower part of the asphalt road, near the *Casa Aixa* shop. **Agulo** is on your left. Look back up at the cliffs you came down and marvel at your achievement! The path is tantalizingly difficult to spot from below.

Visitors' Centre to Las Rosas

From the **Visitors' Centre** you can walk down the winding road, for about 2.5km, into Las Rosas village to the junction where the Vallehermoso-San Sebastián buses stop. They also pick up from the large viewpoint restaurant that is 10-15 minutes walk further from Las Rosas up the Vallehermoso road.

Visitors' Centre to Las Rosas to Roque Cano to Vallehermoso

Walk 7 in reverse is possible from the Visitors' Centre. Leave the Centre to the right by the main, descending asphalt road, and follow this down to a junction, a way above the main road, where an asphalt road leads off up to the left. Follow this road through the upper parts of Las Rosas to emerge by a dam. Cross the dam and turn left. Follow the asphalt road along and up the valley, until just past the multicoloured Camp Laurisilva you take a dirt track off right to Los Zarzales. At a green gate across the track the Roque Cano path goes off left. See **Walk 7**.

5 Vallehermoso to Chorros de Epina

Vallehermoso (186m/610ft) is a large village, with numerous outlying hamlets spread along several ascending valleys. The name means *beautiful valley*, but it is also referred to as the *valley of a thousand palms*. The Canary palm, a native species, is cultivated for palm honey, a dark syrup used on local desserts such as *flan*. Note the footholds or metal climbing pins in some of the taller trees' trunks. Allow about 3 hours to Chorros de Epina.

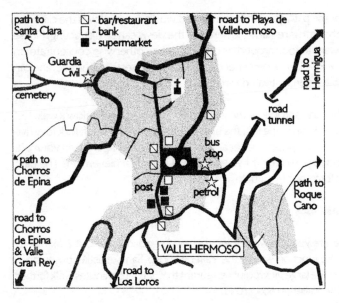

From the main square of Vallehermoso, head up the street to the left of the *Caja Canarias* bank. Just past the butchers (*carniceira Quico*), turn left up a flight of steps. When the path levels out, turn right up a zigzag of steps to the next, asphalt, road, which goes to Valle Gran Rey. Opposite are a water tap and more steps going on upwards to the left, marked with a yellow **H**. Go up these and at a fork, take the left turn up towards a large palm tree and cacti. Pass the top house and their noisy dogs, going just left of the house and round behind a bit of fence, then on up to the ridge. There are views down to the right into the next little valley, the Barranco del Clavo. Head on up left, and follow the path as it zigzags its way along the ridge.

At a rocky corner looking down over the hamlet of La Quilla, a dog may bark noisily. Ignore it and continue up to the right, heading towards the telecom mast. Cross a section of grey cinder path. At a higher point the path dips, though briefly, before the final climb up the ridge and towards the mast. Below the telecom station, the path curves to join a dirt track. Go left on the track, which soon joins the asphalt road.

Right goes to Epina, Alojera and Taguluche villages (**Walks 8 & 10**), but for Chorros de Epina, turn left along the asphalt. (See map). Then, at a junction signposted left to Vallehermoso (11km), turn right. A short distance along on the right is the large *Chorros de Epina* restaurant. Beyond it, take a level dirt track off right to the Ermita of San Isidor. At the ermita a path to the left goes a short distance up into the laurel woodland, another one beyond goes to the Alojera and Taguluche roads, and one on the right goes down to the springs of **Chorros de Epina** (800m/2625ft) and picnic seats just below.

You can return to Vallehermoso by the same route, or by one of the following:

Chorros de Epina to Santa Clara to Vallehermoso

Return on the asphalt, the way you came, but go *left* on the asphalt road to Alojera. Further along the ridge, turn right, onto a dirt track, moments after passing the asphalt right turn to the telecom mast - from where you emerged earlier. This track leads you around the west and northwest side of the ridge. At a fork of the tracks, take the upper route to the right. *Left goes to Arguamul.* Eventually, you will arrive at the **Ermita of Santa Clara**. The direct path to Vallehermoso goes off right before the ermita 'car park' (see part of **Walk 6** in reverse). Alternatively, from Santa Clara you could continue to Buenavista and Playa de Vallehermoso as described in the last three paragraphs of **Walk 6**.

Chorros de Epina to La Meseta to Los Loros to Vallehermoso

A third possible return from Chorros de Epina, is to go with the asphalt back past the restaurant, but instead of turning left, to stay with the main asphalt road down towards Vallehermoso. After several descending curves of the road, you reach the signed *Camino Forestal de la Meseta*. This is a comparatively level dirt track, along the folds below the northern edge of the central plateau. It leads after a couple of kilometres to the edge of some excellent laurel forest. If you are just interested in the laurels, it is suggested that you retrace your steps from here.

The long onward route does not have much to recommend it and the weather is often bad here later in the day. The track continues, eventually, to a small dam and reservoir. From there it is possible to descend by a bad path, near or in the stream bed, to a dirt track above **Los Loros** village. To avoid any ornithological disappointment here, note that the Spanish *Loros* here means *laurels*, not *parrots*. From the village, a long asphalt road leads down, between the friendly locals' houses and vegetable plots, into Vallehermoso.

6 Vallehermoso to Santa Clara to Buenavista to Playa to Vallehermoso

Allow about 4 hours or more. This route involves a continuous descent of 500m towards the end - anyone preferring steep ascents to steep descents may wish to do the route in reverse. From the main square of Vallehermoso, head up the street to the left of the *Caja Canarias* bank. At the end of the narrow street, turn left and join the main Valle Gran Rey road. This swings left at the Guardia Civil, but immediately past here, a track goes off right to the cemetery. Follow this track but turn right onto the footpath immediately before the cemetery gates and take the path down to the footbridge. From the bridge, go between two little buildings, turn right at the fork and head uphill. Follow the zigzags up to the larger house. Turn left in front of, and go up to the left of, the house and where a small path crosses, continue on and upwards. Pass by a water tank on the right, which has a funnel-type entrance underneath.

Ignoring smaller paths down to the left, continue on the straightforward main path along the right-hand side of the valley, the Barranco de la Era Nueva. At a rocky corner, just after a water tank with palms around it, take the right upward turn where a leftward path goes down among the trees. Continue upvalley, in some places along the stream bed. Pass a small side-valley on the left, then the entrance of a much larger side-valley on the same side. Your path zigzags up in the narrowing main valley, now to the left of the streambed. In places it can be quite narrow, with tall vegetation beside it.

At the head of the valley there is a natural bowl or caldera, with cliffs around. Your path zigzags up towards the right-hand side of this, on a loose earth path through scattered laurels, to emerge finally onto a bare earth ridge. From here there are beautiful views of Tenerife and Tamargada village to the right, and the rocky mass of Teselinde peak (876m/2875ft) in front of you. Your onward, rocky path edges around the right hand side of Teselinde and gives further views down into the Barranco de Los Guanches.

On reaching a wide dirt track, the **Ermita of Santa Clara** (720m/2360ft) is on your right and to your left the track goes towards Chorros de Epina. Ahead of you a steep path leads down to Arguamul (part of **Walk 8**, in reverse). As you go to look over at the view, you can hear the sudden roar of the waves breaking on the Arguamul coastal rocks over 700m below. On the coast to the left of Arguamul is the jagged headland of the Punta del Peligro, the *Point of Danger*. The serpentine back of La Palma is visible on the horizon.

> *It is possible to go left from here with the dirt track, then return via part of* **Walk 5** *reversed. Turn left from Santa Clara and follow the track past a huge rocky amphitheatre. It is a long walk, but eventually you will pass a track turning sharply back down right for Arguamul. Continue onwards here until, below the telecom mast, you emerge finally and briefly onto the asphalt of the Epina/Alojera/Taguluche road. Turn left, then almost immediately left again, on the asphalt road to the mast (see* **Walk 5***). Follow this for a distance then, on the outside of a bend, go off right on a descending track. This swings left. Follow it for a short way, then a clear path leads off right. Follow this down to Vallehermoso.*

To go onwards to Buenavista mirador and Playa de Vallehermoso, go to the right at Santa Clara, pass the ermita, and follow the main track. *Alternatively, a pleasant path with good views goes off left from behind the ermita and rejoins the track later.* After a couple of kilometres pass the Ermita of the Virgen de Guadalupe on the right, and then the turning off to the abandoned village of Chiguere on the left. Finally the track ends at the little cone like-hill of **Buenavista** (566m/1 855ft) with wonderful views along the north coast. The postcard-featured **Roques de los Organos** are below you to the left, but their basalt columns are only visible from the sea.

Retrace your steps a short way back down the slope from Buenavista, to find the entrance on your left of the steep path that descends **500m** to Playa de Vallehermoso. This path is a little vertiginous in places, and can be tiring in hot weather. The last few minutes are down a boulder-strewn stream gully and down steps by a house. When you finally reach the asphalt road, the beach with its compelling, boiling sea is left, Vallehermoso is right.

There has been considerable refurbishment work under way at Playa, with stone promenades under construction. It is extremely unlikely that anyone would consider swimming at this beach, but the huge waves against the dark rocks are very dramatic. There is a small bar, popular with the locals. From Playa it is a rather tedious 3km walk back uphill along the asphalt into Vallehermoso, however look out for one of the tallest palm trees on the island. About halfway back from Playa, a new botanical garden is under construction, but progress, like that of the new airport, seems very slow. Back in Vallehermoso, keep left by the *Los Organos* bar to reach the central square.

If doing this walk in reverse, we would suggest a taxi down to Playa de Vallehermoso. Walk a few minutes back uphill to find the signed path to Buenavista.

7 Vallehermoso to Roque Cano to Las Rosas

Allow about 3 hours to Las Rosas. From the central square in Vallehermoso, face the *Amaya* bar/restaurant and go down the street to the left, passing the post office and three supermarkets before reaching a T-junction at the *Garajonay* bar. Go left and down to cross the bridge. Turn right and follow the road up to a corner to the left. Some steps take you up to join the same road as it swings back across the hillside. Turn right onto the road and follow it as it curves left, into a narrow ravine. Turn left onto a slowly-stepped track that leads off just before a terrace wall and is marked with an **H**. Follow this track and go around a corner onto a rock path heading towards **Roque Cano** (630m/2065ft). Where a good branch goes off to the right, you can divert up to a mirador with views over Vallehermoso, but return afterwards to the path and continue onwards.

Continue along the path. There are views down to the right to small reservoirs in the narrow valley. As you round the last corner before the Roque, and head in towards the main cliff face, there are short cuts back up to the right. Ignore these and continue with the main path, which goes almost up to the cliff, then loops up to the right and climbs again.

After passing the Roque, the path swings round onto a more shaded bit of hillside early in the day. There are views to the road tunnel below, to Tamargada village, and to the Buenavista path up from Playa de Vallehermoso. There are scattered heathers and laurels around and a convenient natural stone bench makes a good site for a picnic or refreshments pause.

The wide path crosses from one hill to another by means of a narrow ridge, with lovely views down on either side into the valleys. It then climbs by short sections through tree heather, then later with small areas of laurel overhanging the path. A moment's sidetrack off to the right will take you down to a little knoll with views down to the valleys. Shortly after this knoll, cross a small landslip, using a makeshift path. Not far beyond, there is another viewpoint off to the right.

After a tunnel of tree heather, the path emerges at a sandy corner. From here there is a view south down into a side valley, to numerous terraces on the hillside opposite you and to the few, scattered houses of **El Tion** (380m/1245ft). A ridge path can be seen leading down into the valley on the far side. Emerge onto a dirt track by a green gate marked *Los Zarzales*, and turn right onto the dirt track. At the second turn of the track, there is a small shrine. Continue, and join an asphalt road. Turn left here, with the multicoloured *Camp Laurisilva* on the right. Follow the asphalt along and down the valley to, and across, a dam. At the 4-way junction on the far side of the dam, turn first left and down to the main road in Las Rosas, through a church square with a tiny shop. Alternatively, after the dam, take the second left, a more level asphalt road and follow this across to connect with the Las Rosas-Laguna Grande road where you can turn right for the Visitors' Centre. Note that many houses in Las Rosas have small but somewhat aggressive terriers - presumably due to a local rat problem.

8 Epina to Arguamul to Ermita de Santa Clara to Epina

This walk starts from the Alojera road and goes to the village of Arguamul, which stretches down a remote hillside on the barren north-northeast corner of the island, overlooking the sea and just west of the basalt columns of Los Organos. Allow about 3-4 hours, plus extra time if you want to go down towards the sea at Arguamul. Epina is the nearest village to the start point of the walk, but the walk does not go through it.

The Alojera road starts from the main Vallehermoso-Chorros de Epina road, leaving it a few minutes below the *Chorros de Epina* restaurant (See map). The surfaced road runs northwards, out along a narrow ridge, then cuts left through the spine of the ridge. Immediately before it cuts through, there is an asphalt road off right, going onto the east side of the ridge and to a conspicuous transmitter mast. (**Walk 5** comes in here.) Moments later, on the west side of the ridge, a dirt road goes off right, signed for Tazo and Arguamul, and is the start of the walk (800m/2625ft).

Go off the asphalt and onto this dirt road, heading northwards. The road runs around two huge curves of the hillside, to reach in about 30 minutes, a junction. Here, there is a semi-legible sign indicating uphill, right, for Chiguere and Santa Clara. The scattered houses of Tazo village **(Walk 9)** are visible below you to the left. Go left at the junction, downhill, and stay with the road in a generally northeasterly direction.

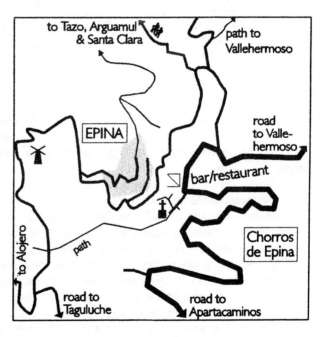

After a small cutting,
the dirt road swings back to the left by an abandoned shed. Before going left with the road, walk a short way on and past the shed for a view down to the north coast. To the

left, the spectacular Cerro de Bejira ridge runs into the sea at the Punta del Peligro (*Danger Point*). Arguamul village is out of sight around to the right. Return to the road and descend to the junction below, to turn right for Arguamul. This road crosses the ridge at about 500m altitude, then swings right and along the north face of the steep slope. From here on, the road clings precariously but spectacularly to the hillside, particularly where it cuts in deeply to the right to negotiate the Barranco de la Higuera.

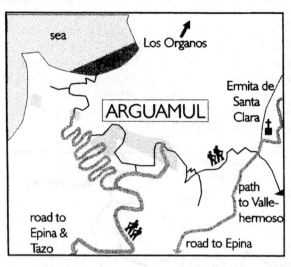

Stay with the road (you have little alternative!).

Soon the power tower of **Arguamul** comes into view, above a junction in the road. From this junction, the left fork descends, eventually to reach lower Arguamul at about 190m altitude. The right goes to the upper part of the village at about 460m, with another 50m of Arguamul above it. Take the upper fork, and most of the village comes into view. Follow the road towards the village, but look out for a marked path heading down to the left, with accompanying street lamps.

If you want to see the lower parts of the village or Arguamul's rocky beach, go down this path and then left, at the junction just below. Follow the path downhill, much of it paved and walled, towards lower Arguamul. Descending, the path forks. There is a choice of straight on beside a small house, or swinging to the right behind the vine terraces. Go right, down towards a house with a flat green roof, and continue to the right of it. The path drops, finally to join the newer dirt track (the left fork from the power tower high above). Go right onto the track. You may locate some surviving sections of the old, stony path, between the zigzags of the new track, though not all sections are easily accessible.

The dirt track ends at a little cluster of houses, Arguamul's lowest but still high above the sea. Just before the end of the track, a path off right between the houses is signed to '*Playa*'. Follow this path and emerge from the back of the little settlement, on a path that winds around a small rocky outcrop with a pool. Continue down to a fork, where right goes down to the stony beach, or left goes down towards the sea rocks. The choice is yours.

Return by the same route, but instead of turning right onto the final section of path to rejoin the upper dirt road, stay left on the path and go round to the left of the village. A final, hand-railed stretch takes you up to join the end of the access dirt road.

If you do not want to make the descent to and ascent from lower Arguamul, stay on the access dirt road to the end.

From the end of the road, a path continues up steps. Mostly it stays on the left-hand side of the upper village ridge, but simply follow the street lamps up. From the very top of the village, continue, climbing to a junction by a shaded spring. Here an old, broad path goes on to the right, but take the zigzag path up left. The cross of Santa Clara is soon visible on the skyline to the left. The path rises to a concrete water-control building, but you go to the left just before this.

Your route runs on, under a cliff, then winds up across an area of bare yellow earth. Try to stay with the established zigzags here, rather than using the steeper shortcuts, as the earth on the latter is very loose. The path finally brings you to join a level dirt road, with the **Ermita of Santa Clara** (720m/2360ft) on the left, and the path to Vallehermoso (part of **Walk 6**, in reverse) disappearing into the bushes ahead.

Turn right on the dirt road, and follow this to the Chiguere-Santa Clara junction of your outward route, from where you should go on left, and back to your starting point.

9 Epina to Tazo to Cubada to Alojera

Allow at least 2 hours. Epina is the nearest village to the start point of the walk, but the walk does not go through it. The walk starts at the same point as **Walk 8** on the Alojera road and goes to the village of Tazo, which is situated in a valley in the northeast corner of the island. It continues to Alojera, a larger, more scattered village, connected by a long asphalt road to Epina. There are at least two taxis based in Alojera, although they are not guaranteed to be there when you want them. It may be possible to hitch a lift from Alojera back towards Chorros de Epina or Vallehermoso.

The Alojera road starts from the main Vallehermoso-Chorros de Epina road, leaving it a few minutes below the *Chorros de Epina* restaurant. The surfaced road runs northwards, out along a narrow ridge, then cuts left through the spine of the ridge. Immediately before it cuts through, there is an asphalt road off right, going onto the east side of the ridge and to a conspicuous transmitter mast. (**Walk 5** comes in here.) Moments later, on the west side of the ridge, a dirt road goes off right, signed for Tazo and Arguamul, and is the start of the walk (800m/2625ft). See map.

Go off the asphalt and onto this dirt road, heading northwards. The road runs around a huge curve of the hillside, before cornering around a ridge. From this corner, an initially clear path goes up right and down left. Go left and follow the zigzag path down. It is vague in places, but it will bring you down to a T-junction with a better path below.

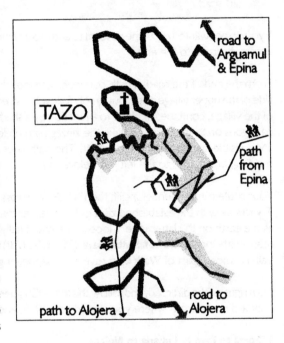

This second path has been visible for some time, below but parallel with the road. Go right and follow the path down into the next fold of the hillside. Before it starts to climb the following ridge, which has a large pylon down to the left, the path crosses a line of palm trees. Immediately *after* these palms, a clear path goes off to the left. Take this and head towards the pylon.

If you have missed the start of the first path, the road will bring you to the Chiguere-Santa Clara junction. Go left on the road, but immediately past the junction, turn back left on a black path. Follow this down, and as you come in line with the pylon and the ridge, you should see a path branching off right to going just left of the pylon. Take this.

The two paths join just below the pylon, which is reached by the first route in about half an hour from the start. The path now takes you down-ridge towards the next pylon and Tazo village. Nearer **Tazo**, the path loops back right, then left, above an agave-filled gully. Ten minutes from the first pylon, you arrive at the top of the village, just above the top house (410m/1345ft), where the path forks. Take the main route to the right, which emerges onto a dirt track just beyond the house. Go left. A short way along, at a junction, go onwards, to the right of a house. Swing round to the right and follow the track. Where it ends, by a house, turn left to join a path with street-lamps. At the bottom of this path, turn right onto a dirt road. Follow the road through the village, and turn left at the first proper junction of roads, with a big house on the left. Follow the road out of the village.

Below the village, where a very straight walled-path crosses the road, go right, down this path. It brings you to a lower section of the road where you should cross over and continue on the path. Cross the dirt road for a second time and rejoin the path. As the path nears a junction of stream beds, the walls end and it zigzags down over black volcanic rock. You can probably see the onward path, as it climbs up the far bank of the left-hand stream bed.

Before reaching the junction of the stream beds, go down to the left. Cross the stream and go up underneath an overhanging rock, then right and onto the path, about 20 minutes from Tazo. Cross a little ridge and the main dirt road comes into sight on the left. There is an obvious connecting track between the dirt road and your path, but join this connecting track and go *right*, away from the road. Ignore cairns to the left here.

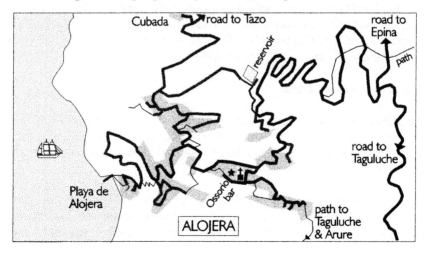

Follow the small track to the end of the ridge where it zigzags down and narrows to a path. This path runs down to the right along a little streambed, with high terrace walls on the right. Pass a water tank built into the far right hillside. The path swings left and takes you to the streambed.

Go up the far side of the stream bed, to the right, where you join a good path towards the sea. This forks moments later, where you take the upper path. Approaching a row of four palm trees, the path forks again. Go left, down a deeply excavated path beside the trees, then right onto terraces again. Less than a minute later, the path doglegs down left in the direction of the streambed. A path comes in from the right, but continue down towards the stream. Cross the streambed diagonally and go up the far side. Arrive at the houses of **Cubada** hamlet (130m/425ft) and take the track up to the left of them.

Go right at a junction onto the dirt road and within five minutes of Cubada, enter a long narrow valley. Loop around this and follow the main track to join the asphalt in **Alojera** near a bar/shop, just over an hour from Tazo.

Stay with the asphalt and, at the next junction, go left and wind uphill with the road towards the main part of Alojera. The road goes sharply right and the first house on the right is that of a taxi-driver (tel.: 800259). The road then swings back left, passing first a tall, isolated house by the corner, then a new house. Just after the road swings left again, a path, marked by a street lamp, goes up to the right. Follow this path, which joins the end of a road, which will lead you up to the *Ossorio* bar, the school, and church (230m/755ft). There are also a couple of small shops here. A left turn beyond the church, will bring you down to the main road. The last house on the left before the main road is that of another taxi-driver. The main road runs uphill to the right, to Epina and then the Vallehermoso-Chorros de Epina road.

Path up to Chorros de Epina

This path connects the Taguluche/Alojera-Epina road with Chorros de Epina, cutting off a long loop of road near the modern windmills. The route starts just under 1 km north of the Alojera/Taguluche junction, although it is now the continuation of a new path coming up from the Alojera direction.

Turn uphill onto the path, and after 3-4 minutes, ignore a fork off to the left. After about 15 minutes from the road, pass a water tank and go onto a steeper and damper, tree-lined path. About three minutes later, arrive at the ermita at Chorros de Epina. *Go down* and left just beyond the ermita if you want to see the springs. A sign explains the legend, so you may wish to sample the waters. Return to the ermita. Take the main dirt track beyond the church, and in about five minutes arrive at the asphalt road. The *Chorros de Epina* restaurant is a short way down on the left.

10 Alojera to Taguluche

This walk follows an easy path uphill from the top of Alojera to cross the asphalt road into Taguluche, where it crosses the dramatic Galión ridge which separates the two villages. Allow about 30 minutes for this section. From the road a path descends through an empty valley to Taguluche's isolated Ermita de Santo. This path is not well surfaced, steep in places, and requires both care and agility. Allow about 1 hour for the downhill section to Taguluche.

The walk starts from the main church in **Alojera**, (near the school and *Ossorio* bar). See Alojera map for details of finding the start point. From the T-junction immediately inland of the church, with the main road below and behind you, go left, uphill and inland, on the surfaced road. Follow this road up through high parts of the village. Where the asphalt ends, go right in front of the power tower and the nearest pylon. Cross an area of black volcanic rock, and reach, in about three minutes, a palm-filled stream bed. Over the stream, there is a junction of paths and you should go up to the left. Follow the path up the nose of the ridge, along a series of zigzags, to finally emerge onto the asphalt road to Taguluche.

On the far side of the road is the start of the uphill path to Arure (part of **Walk II**, in reverse), but go right on the road a short distance to the corner on the inland end of the dramatic Galión ridge which separates Alojera and Taguluche.

From the corner of the road, head out seawards onto the Galión and look for a large cairn marking a path to the *right*. Do not go *up* the first little peak ahead, but to the right of it. Follow the path to a saddle beyond the little peak, where another cairn marks the start of the Taguluche path. Go left. The first section of the path is narrow and stony, and some care is necessary. It does get a little wider as it nears some large cliffs, and then starts to zigzag down. After the zigzag, the path crosses a sill of red rock and then levels out along the hillside.

After a particularly narrow section of earth path, the path zigzags downwards a little more, and a spectacular tall and jagged sill of red rock comes into view. The path becomes more level again for a stretch under huge dark cliffs. Go carefully around a little gate-like wall that is positioned across the path. Continue on, with a little palm-filled side-valley coming in from the right. Within a minute of the gate-wall, you should swing back left, off the old path and onto a boulder-strewn little path, to a lower cairn. The path zigzags down, and below you, angular sills give the impression of a ruined fortress. There are some vague stretches of path here, but look out for the cairns and they will guide you down towards the fortress. A rock wall looms in front of your path. You should zigzag down to the left of it, then just below it go right.

The entrance to the fortress is marked by a little gate, though this is not intended to be opened. Climb around the left of it, being careful of the wires. A further, gravelly slope brings you down to a huge section of wall. Pass to the left of a breach in this wall. At this point, a view of the island of Hierro may be neatly framed by the barranco walls ahead. Below this section of wall, the stream bed comes through from the right and drops to the main valley bed. Head down to the stream bed, then go down it cautiously. Swing to the right before the drop, onto a narrow little path.

Make your way down to the main valley bed and cross this right-diagonally, to the far bank. Go up a faint path, behind a jagged tooth of rock. On the southern side of the barranco, the path is mostly more straightforward, although it is still narrow and is loosely surfaced in places, and care is still necessary. It climbs to negotiate a black gully, then levels out a little. Around a corner, about 45 minutes down from the road, arrive at a spectacular view of Taguluche's Ermita de San Salvador. The path leads you to this church in a further ten minutes. Turn left through the church courtyard and onto the asphalt road for the rest of **Taguluche**. **Walk 12** describes the route from Taguluche, via the *Alto Camino*, to Valle Gran Rey.

11 Arure to Alojera

Arure (820m/2690ft) is the first village on the *Cumbre* or central plateau, once you emerge from the Barranco del Valle Gran Rey. Allow about 70 minutes.

At the beginning of the village, the track to the mirador is signed, leaving the main asphalt road beside a pink house. Follow this track past a few houses. (A co-financed tunnel has been put through the ridge to below the existing mirador and, when finished, will alter the route to it.) Take a stepped track up right and go under an arch. The Taguluche valley opens up spectacularly in front of and below you. To the right, beyond Taguluche village, is the jagged ridge of Galión. Turn right to the Ermita de Santo, and go beyond onto an earth path. After a short way a path breaks off left to descend the cliffs steeply, the route down to Taguluche **(Walk 12)**, but stay with the main path to the right.

Follow the path through several broad curves as it runs under and along the cliff faces. At the end of the cliffs, the steep slope of the edge of the *Cumbre* swings away to the right. A little col brings you to a sudden view of the cultivated area of Alojera, and the modern windmills of Epina.

From the col, a zigzag path takes you briefly through the edge of a little pinewood. Beyond the pines, look back up left for some spectacular eroded lichenous rocks. Much

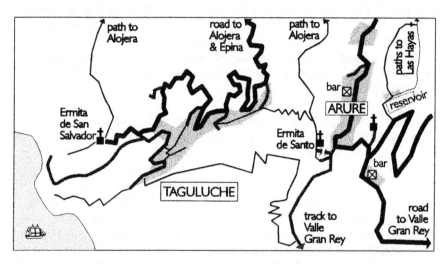

of the onward, downward path is visible, going towards a single pylon in the centre of a loop of road. At a fork in a rocky area, you should go down and right, rather than back and left. Make a zigzag down past spiny agave plants and then the path levels out on the ridge for a short while. As you head towards the pylon, a path goes back down left, but you should go straight on, down the ridge, to the pylon. Once well below the pylon, ignore a small path heading back down left in the Taguluche direction. Continue, to reach the road in about 15 minutes from the col.

From the road you could go down the Galión path to Taguluche **(Walk 21)**, but for the onward route to Alojera, cross over the road, where cairned, and follow the path opposite. Descend along the ridge, soon on a series of zigzags. The path comes down to a palm-filled stream bed and a junction of paths in about 12 minutes from the road.

Go right, across the little stream, and the path takes you out of the palm valley to an area of black volcanic rock. About three minutes after the stream, pass a house, and the path finally emerges beside a power tower and a pylon at the top end of an asphalt road. Turn left onto the road and head downhill. At a junction just before the main church in **Alojera**, go right and past a small shop, down to the main road. Alternatively, go left, past the church, school and *Ossorio* bar, then follow the street/path to join the main road lower in the village.

12 Arure to Taguluche to La Merica to Valle Gran Rey (La Calera)

Valle Gran Rey is Gomera's busiest resort, set at the mouth of the huge eponymous barranco. Vueltas and La Playa are the two main villages on the coast, with older La Calera a short distance inland. Behind La Calera are another 3km of the barranco, with smaller hamlets and much terraced cultivation. Allow at least 5 hours for the walk, since there are two long, steep descents and one long ascent, totalling some 2000m change of altitude.

Arure (820m/2690ft) is the first village once you emerge from the Barranco del Valle Gran Rey. At the beginning of the village, the track to the mirador is signed, leaving the main asphalt road beside a pink house. Follow this track past a few houses. (A co-financed tunnel has been put through the ridge to below the existing mirador and, when finished, will alter the route to it.) Take a stepped track up right and go under an arch. The Taguluche valley opens up spectacularly in front of you. Part of your return path is visible as a zigzag up the cliffs to the left of centre. To the right, beyond Taguluche, is the jagged ridge of Galión. Turn right to the Ermita de Santo, and go beyond onto an earth path. After a short way a path breaks off left to descend the cliffs steeply - this is your way down to Taguluche. The top half, with some deep rock steps, is the most vertiginous, but the second half is in worse condition, with some damp slippery sections near brambles.

The path emerges in **Taguluche** (200m/655ft), by what appear to be the village's highest, but ruined, house, and its uppermost lamp standard. Take the path that zigzags downwards to the left of the asphalt road, almost following the lamp standards. At a T-junction of the dirt track, with two descending options, go down to the right. Join the asphalt, then go left downhill. At present the asphalt ends at the white power-tower, and continues as steps going down from the side of the tower. Follow the steps and subsequent pathways, and you may find the telltale crates of empty bottles and thus the small block building which is a tiny café. Go left at the café and steps bring you down to the asphalt road. Follow the asphalt down to the west, towards the sea. Just before the end of this section of asphalt, by a parking place, concrete steps lead up to the left, beside a large water pipe. This is the start of your onward route, back up the hillside and on to La Merica.

A path continues, beyond the end of the asphalt, right down to the sea, but this adds another 100m descent and 100m ascent back...

Follow the concrete steps and path. Just past a house on the right, the onward path breaks off the main path and rises steeply to the left beside another house. It is easy to go wrong here. This route is known locally as the *Alto Camino*, "high road", if you need to ask. At a crossing of the paths, take the middle, most upward one. Once past this immediate area, the path is clear as it runs across the lower hillside, separated from the village to the north by a streambed.

Higher up, where the streambed reaches the same level as the path, go left to cross the stream and follow an obvious path uphill. Continue straight on, upwards. Further up, ignore a side-path going off left onto the terraces. The path climbs. At junctions follow the most obvious one upwards. Pass, on your left, a dried-up gully bed. As the gully steepens, so does the path. Climb to an eroded section of earth, where a steep path continues onwards in the gully bed itself, but take a turning back to the right and up. At a T-junction a path comes in through the gully on your left, from an area almost taken over by prickly-pear cacti, and runs off to your right. Head off right under a low palm tree. You will see the path stretching up on the hillside in front of you. At a T-junction take the more obvious path to the left. Look out for a little concrete building, beyond the gully to your left. Moments after, your path turns right. At a higher, leftward bend you can look down and see a small forest of pine trees in the gully to your right.

The path comes out onto open hillside and starts to curve slowly round to the right. Look higher up and see an area of reddish cliff, with pine trees, almost towards the top of the ridge. The path goes up towards these trees, then climbs through the pine woodland, and then onto a stone staircase up an open cliff face towards the seemingly impenetrable ridge. Finally you pass through the ridge via a door-width cutting, to a completely different, but spectacular, view down to the sea and a pointed rock.

After the previous, dramatic route, an anticlimactic path winds on up the hillside to your left. Join a dirt track. Arure is to the left, and to the right is the route to La Merica and Valle Gran Rey. The track to the right is built-up on a retaining wall at first and passes some beehives, before heading down the ridge.

Head on towards the more pointed bits of the ridge, as the main dirt track swings right and dead-ends at a rubbish-tip. Take the left turn here, before the tip, along the left side of the ridge. Ahead of you, you can see that the route forks. You will be taking the upper, right-hand steps and path, towards the top of the trees on the skyline. This junction is obvious when you reach it as the steps are marked with a yellow **H** and a large black **VALLE GRAN REY** arrow. The path climbs and goes around to a ridge with spectacular views of the sea and, unfortunately, of Valle Gran Rey's huge rubbish landslide.

Follow the path along the main ridge, with a possible short detour up to the obvious **La Merica** trig point (850m/2790ft) and cliff views. Pass a partly collapsed house, a pathside lime kiln and a slaking pit, to reach the descent zigzag above Valle Gran Rey. Here two paths off to the right run along to a mirador, but take the downward path which zigzags for approximately **600m** into upper La Calera village. During the second half of the descent, ignore two reasonable-looking paths that branch off to the right. Stay on the main path, which will, eventually, zigzag down above a distinctive, large semi-triangular water tank among the houses. Join the higher asphalt road of La Calera and turn right. At the shop *Tienda Victor*, turn left down the steps.

For the reverse route up La Merica, to find the path from La Calera, join the asphalt road through the La Calera village proper (not the main through road to Playa and Vueltas) and head inland. At an asphalt turning up to the left - marked with a 'no entry' sign - La Galeria is up above you on the left. Go left with the road. Look out for the water tank on your right, then look left to where, just off the road, a gully is bridged and the path goes off and up to the left. It is signposted with a wooden board.

13 Apartacaminos to Las Creces to Las Hayas to El Cercado to Valle Gran Rey

Apartacaminos (1020m/3345ft) is the 3-way junction of roads to Valle Gran Rey, to Vallehermoso, and to the central ridge. The Valle Gran Rey-San Sebastián bus will stop here. Allow five hours for this walk. For shorter versions with less, or no, time in the forest, you could start at the Jardín de las Creces track*, or at Las Hayas

At Apartacaminos, turn onto the central ridge road, the Carretera Dorsal (or del Centro), follow it and then turn right onto a track at a sign for *Cañadas del Jorge*. This track goes through damp, lichenous, laurel woodland, then into slightly drier heather and faya woodland.

The track swings round to the left and descends into lower, heather woodland. At a junction marked with a signpost for the *Cañada de Jorge/Carretera Dorsal*, turn left. (Right goes to Arure in 2.1 km, and to Las Hayas - see at end of this walk.) This path winds and climbs back through the woodland to rejoin the main road opposite a picnic site by a *Raso de Bruma* sign. Beyond the picnic site, the northern slope of the island ridge drops away steeply towards Vallehermoso, though this is not obvious because of the density of the trees.

Turn right onto the asphalt, and follow the road until a turning right onto a track signed *Camino Forestal Jardín de las Creces**. Follow this track through woodland, to a large picnic site. At the barbecues area, swing right onto the exit dirt track with a chain barrier.

(Alternatively, follow the recently-constructed, numbered Creces trail, signposted to Las Creces. Go left, where Arure is signed 2.6km to the right. Emerge at the crossroads* below)

The exit track from the barbecues runs along the left-hand side of a deepening, stream gully. Stay with the track until it passes a sign back to *Carretera Dorsal 1.9km*, then a crossroads* with a path off left signed *Las Hayas 0.7km*. Go left and follow the path through woodland, to emerge to the right of a water tank. Go down to the right of the churchyard just below, then down immediately left of a telegraph pole and right of a green-netting fence, to reach the asphalt road in **Las Hayas** (1030m/3380ft), opposite the *Montaña* restaurant. The village has another bar/restaurant, the *Amparo*, up the asphalt to the left. **Walk 16** goes from here into Valle Gran Rey by a steeper and more direct route.

From the *Montaña* car-park, go between the eucalyptus trees and left to join the concrete path below. Follow the path, which swings round to reach the far side of the valley, where there are palm trees on the terraces. On a low ridge, pass a house on the right, cross a dirt track, and go down some white-edged concrete steps. At a walled fork, take the left-hand path, ignoring a yellow **H** marking the path to the right. The path narrows and takes you uphill past some dead palm trees, with a fence on the right. There is a view back to the island of La Palma, in the distance above Las Hayas.

Reach a cross-paths with a view to El Cercado village and beyond it to flat-topped Mount Fortaleza. Go straight across here and your path then swings around to the left, to the rim of the Barranco del Agua. Follow a short path along the cliff, passing a water tank, and your route then drops into a hanging valley. This is the upper part of the barranco, and separated from the main part by a huge wall of rock. Cross the streambed and go up on the far side.

The path crosses another streambed, then climbs on a paved staircase to the right. After a distance up the hillside, the original path splits off to the left but runs parallel with the new for a little while. Take this older path. It soon swings left, then emerges higher, and rather scruffily, into the corner of **El Cercado** village (1040m/3410ft), by *Maria's* café. Your onward route goes along the dirt track off right from the road, opposite the café.

However, before you follow it, you may like to go on a short way, around the corner of the road. Have a look at the main part of the village where there is a second bar, the Vitoria, two potteries (producing hand-thrown pottery) and, further on in the village, a tiny shop/bar.

Go along the dirt track whose entrance is opposite *Maria's*. As you near the last few houses, you can see both Hierro and La Palma islands. After the final building, the track drops as it goes along the ridge. At the lowest point, before it starts to rise again, a track goes off, running back down to the left towards the lower part of the village valley. Your path leads off to the right, where the main track starts to rise again. A sign marks the start of the proper path, though other small paths lead off right before it.

Stay with the path as it descends diagonally the slope towards Valle Gran Rey, winding around the folds of the hillside. This is a long section of path, but a very varied one with changing views. In a few places the path's surface is a little steep and loose, but it is mostly reasonable. Botanists will find the pathside flora interesting here.

Eventually, nearing civilization, the path goes to the right of a row of short palm-trees and becomes well-paved steps. It drops to join a good terrace path coming in from the right. Turn down left. This junction is marked with a red **O** and an arrow. Just above the asphalt road, you can turn either left or right to join it, but go left. Once on the road, by the water channel, go left with the asphalt. **Walk 18** comes in from the left shortly afterwards.

You can turn right, soon after, onto a stepped path which will take you down to the valley floor. Cross the barranco bed between tall reeds and then follow the path out as it swings gradually left and emerges by the school. A bright orange building nearby is a good marker from the far side of the valley. Follow the path out to reach the main road and bus route. Left is towards the sea.

At a road junction, turn left, instead of down back to the right. The road swings back inland at the *Bar la Vizcaina* then, shortly afterwards, back towards the sea. Join the path at the end of the asphalt and follow it seaward. Just past a deep gully with a small concrete dam, ignore small paths off left, then a steep descent to the right. The main path goes around to a church courtyard, the **Ermita de los Reyes**. Cross the courtyard and continue on the old, stepped path, which zigzags down to the valley floor below the church. At the floor of the barranco, cross the dirt track. Your path continues onwards to cross the lowest bit of the barranco bed. Turn left at a wall and head up the steps, then follow the road down left to Valle Gran Rey.

Cañada de Jorge to Jorge/Las Creces junction

About 11 minutes. From the Cañada de Jorge junction **(Walk 9)**, signed right to Arure 2.1 km, go right. Follow the broad path that winds down into a broad valley, with some houses of Arure visible to the left of centre. At a 3-way junction signed left to Las Creces, go left for Las Hayas **(Walk 24)** or go right towards Arure **(Walk 14** in reverse)

14 Arure to Jorge/Las Creces Junction

This walk crosses the plateau northwest of Arure, in about 25 minutes, to a junction for (Cañada de) Jorge and Las Creces/Las Hayas. See the end of this walk for the connexion to **Walk 13**, at Jorge. See **Walk 15** for the onward route to Las Hayas.

Head out from **Arure** along the main road in the direction of Valle Gran Rey. Near the low point of the valley, a track goes off left to the church. Ignore this, but shortly beyond, turn left onto the asphalt road to Las Hayas. As the road climbs, a dam and small reservoir are visible down on the left. Look for a path, going down left from the road towards houses, and take it. Cross the area below the dam and then turn right to go along the shore, beyond the last house to a flattish rocky area. Turn left, inland, to join a clear path above the rocks and follow this uphill to the left of the ridge.

Arure village is across the valley to the left, with cultivation in the valley below. Stay with the path along the side of the Arure valley and towards a small dam and reservoir. Below the dam is a waterfall. On reaching the dam, cross to the far bank and follow the dirt track to the right.

> Alternatively, instead of crossing the dam, it is possible to take the dirt track along the right-hand side of the reservoir. At the end of the track, join the main track and turn right.

At about 25 minutes from the asphalt Las Hayas road, reach a junction of dirt tracks, signed left for (Cañada de) Jorge, and right for Las Creces (and Las Hayas, **Walk 24**).

Jorge/Las Creces junction to Cañada de Jorge

About 20 minutes. At the Jorge/Las Creces junction, from Arure, go left. The track climbs, to pass a well-fenced enclosure patrolled by noisy guard dogs. Once well up into tall scrub, a secondary track swings off to the right, but you should continue left. Moments later, the track splits, with several paths going off to centre and left, but follow the track to the right. Within a couple of minutes you will pass the Parque Garajonay entrance sign and the vegetation changes from scrub to laurel/heather woodland. A few minutes later, you reach a set of signs at a junction (**Walk 9**). Back goes to Arure 2.1 km, left goes to the Carretera Dorsal 1.6km, and onwards to Cañada de Jorge 0.3km (and also to the Carretera Dorsal).

15 Arure to Las Hayas

Allow about 1 hour. Follow **Walk 14** from **Arure** to the Jorge/Las Creces junction, and go right, on the Las Creces track. Ignore a right-angle, fenced track going off left, but at the next junction where the track splits, go off to the left. This track narrows to a broad path after passing a little house. The path stays to the left-hand side of the valley. Pass between vineyards, and ignore a stony path going off right, across the stream. Your path runs on, and joins the end of a dirt track that will take you to the edge of the laurel forest. A path left, in the narrowed valley, goes to Las Creces, but stay with the track, uphill. Cross a chain barrier, and continue on the main track which swings back right above the main valley you have just left.

At a junction about 20 minutes from the Jorge/Creces junction, go left. Your onward track is on the right of a low ridge, with a low valley and a second ridge off to your right. Fortaleza comes into view. The sandy track swings slightly to the right and heads downhill. In sight of Las Hayas, ignore a side track off to the right. Just before the village there is a right-angle track off right, but ignore this. At a cross-ways, just before the asphalt road, a track to the right joins the road, but take the path straight on to emerge near the *Montaña* restaurant.

16 Las Hayas to Valle Gran Rey (Lomo del Balo) to Las Hayas

A circular route from Las Hayas (1030m/3380ft), involving a long descent and ascent. Allow about 3-4 hours. It would be possible to do the descent, and then catch the public bus either back to Las Hayas, or to the sea at Valle Gran Rey. Another alternative would be to start in the Valle Gran Rey valley at the bottom of the ascent, go up to Las Hayas, then descend again, by reversing the two halves of the following walk

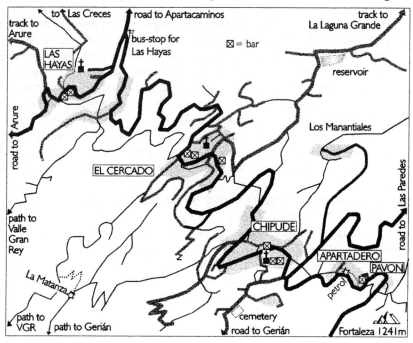

description. 'Haya' is an alternate name for 'faya' (Myrica faya), one of the most abundant laurels, particularly around the edges of the forest and in degraded areas. The small fruits, edible in times of adversity, are known as 'creces'.

If travelling to the start of the walk by public bus, this drops off at the junction of the El Cercado/Chipude road, outside Las Hayas. Walk down the Las Hayas road, passing an asphalt road up right to the church. Pass the *Amparo* bar/restaurant on the left and then a few minutes later, arrive at the eucalyptus-shaded car-park of the older *Montaña* restaurant.

The walk starts in **Las Hayas**, below the eucalyptus trees at the *Montaña*. Follow the path, soon earth-surfaced, then descending across a stream bed. From here, it climbs and swings right, around the back of the valley. Stay with the main path up onto the ridge and cross over the ridge track, passing houses. Go down the concrete steps opposite, then, at a junction about one minute later, go level to the right rather than up to the left (**Walk 13**, to El Cercado, goes left). The rocky-based path soon starts to descend gently into the valley. Stay with the broadest main path, rather than side paths.

As the route nears the rim (1000m/3280ft) of the huge and deep Barranco de Agua, a short path detours off left for a spectacular view into and across this barranco to El Cercado village. Beyond is Chipude village, with flat-topped Fortaleza distinctive on the skyline. Do not follow the cairns on this detour down into the barranco, but return to the main, much wider path, which runs just to the left of the top of the ridge. The path goes uphill with views back to much of Las Hayas, and further views of El Cercado and Chipude. Garajonay summit may be visible. Below you the villages of upper Valle Gran Rey come into view. You can see a path (part of **Walk 9**) climbing down on the far side of the barranco to your left. At about 950m, when your path starts to descend steeply to the left, a red arrow marks a more level detour off to the right, but do not take this.

Stay with the main descending path, through many curves and zigzags. At the foot of the top, cliff section of the valley wall, the path straightens out and heads off down a ridge, though still steeply. Over to the right, the main Valle Gran Rey-Arure road can be seen, climbing from the Valle Gran Rey suburbs of Retamal and Los Granados to the main tunnel. Higher still, the bunker-like greystone mirador restaurant is visible, wedged into the face of the ridge. A smaller, asphalt road connects the main road with the built-up areas in the northeast end of the valley, to your left.

When you are not far above this smaller road, your path forks. Go left, down a stepped path, to join a terrace path running alongside a grey waterpipe. (This junction is after and *below* a path with an open water channel.) Follow the terrace path, with the waterpipe on the right and palm trees on the left, and the asphalt road below left. By a lamp-post and a house, join a raised, paved path. At the bottom of this, turn right on the asphalt. Even after the considerable descent into the Valle Gran Rey valley, you are still at an altitude of about 450m (1475ft) above the sea.

Pass the *Lomo del Balo* bar on your left. The asphalt runs down to join the main Valle Gran Rey-Arure road, but just before it does so it crosses a concrete stream bridge and swings to the left. To the right of and before the bridge, a faint path leads off by a stone wall, and a large boulder. This is the steep, sometimes vertiginous, route back to Las Hayas. The path is not as well built nor as well maintained as the one on which you descended. It can be very hot, with little shade, except later in the day.

The route curves up to the right under the palm trees, on grey boulders. Follow the stream bed up a short way, until the path swings up out of it and to the left. Go back, further left, under a huge palm-tree, and then right again, well above the stream, climbing steeply between terrace walls. The path gains height rapidly, and zigzags up the cliff face, with occasional but brief level stretches.

Finally, the top of the barranco (de las Hayas) comes into sight. Emerge from the valley, before its end, at about 850m altitude, climbing up over the left-hand ridge. A cairned path takes you up to a T-junction with an older, wider, very stony, path. Go right. At a junction with a dirt track, go left, uphill. This track brings you to a corner of the asphalt road, after passing an isolated new house. Go right and follow the road along to Las Hayas. Once the village comes into sight, the tall eucalyptus trees of the *Montaña* restaurant can be seen towards the top of it.

As you enter **Las Hayas**, the road swings right and up, between palm trees. It then makes a loop to the left, but look out to the right, partway along, for a rough uphill path that cuts off the long corner. Go onto the path, then right and back onto the asphalt to arrive at the *Montaña* restaurant moments later.

17 Vueltas to La Calera to Ermita de los Reyes to El Guro to La Playa

A route around the lower half of the Valle Gran Rey barranco, intended as a not-too-strenuous introduction to the area, which can be made circular by returning along the coast to Vueltas. If you're staying in Valle Gran Rey somewhere other than Vueltas, simply join at the appropriate place en route.

Starting from Vueltas harbour, with the beach and harbour behind you, head northwest along the coastal road which runs between the coastal-defence-wall and Vueltas itself. At the roundabout go left with the shoreline. Just before reaching the little Charco del Conde beach, turn inland onto the surfaced road by the *Bajo del Alto* apartments. At the end of the road, just before it swings to the right, take a dirt track going off to the left and follow this. It narrows to a path and goes to the right of a big volcanic rock outcrop. Stay with the main path - bananas on the left, giant reeds on the right. At a fork, go with a bigger dirt track to the right, to emerge by the *Laurisilva* apartments.

On reaching the asphalt road, go across into a small side street to the right of a tourist office. Follow this street gently uphill for a short distance. At the top of the street there are two branches back to the right – the top longer, the bottom shorter – but continue on, past the *Villa Aurora* pension. Turn left into a small footpath. At the junction by the entrance to the *Borbolán* apartments go down to the left past the *El Palmar* bar/restaurant. Turn right onto the first, old road, which runs parallel to the new road beyond. Join the pavement of the new road soon after, where the old road disappears, and continue inland.

Turn right onto another asphalt road, and at the end follow round to the left, into the river bed where you turn right. Stay with the stony river bed, going under a pipe bridge and keeping right on the clear dirt track. Cross a chain, pass a scrapyard, and then go

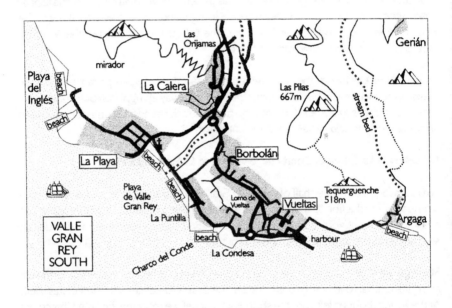

to the right of a cylindrical cement hopper. A few minutes further up the valley, where the track swings to the left to cross the river bed, a small path is cairned going steeply on up the valley wall to the right. This path takes you along the hillside to the courtyard of the Ermita de los Reyes.

At a junction just beyond the church, go steeply down steps to the left (**Walk 16 b** goes level and right). Join a track, beyond an electrical building, and go left and back down valley. Moments later, turn right onto a path, mostly paved, that crosses the valley floor. A quick zigzag takes you up, to the left of a water channel and onto a red earth track. Follow this in front of houses to a paved path that leads to the road.

Turn right for the waterfall, then take the first of two paths off to the left. A short distance along this good path, leave it to go up to the right, where signed. The path goes round to the side valley which runs down from Arure. Once you reach the stream bed, follow it to the right, either beside or in it, on reasonably obvious paths, to arrive at the small waterfall in about 15 minutes. Returning, initially by the same route, look out for a path that comes in from the right, dropping down through the mouth of a deep side valley - this is just before a large water tank. Go up and right on this path, which then swings left and goes to the right of the tank. Ten minutes along top path brings you to the houses El Guro. Turn left, then right at obvious junctions to emerge just before the Associated café.

For El Guro, but not the waterfall, turn left on the main road. As the road bends further to the left, it widens to allow space for car parking on the left. Look on the right of the road and you will see an obvious path going up into the area of houses on the hillside. El Guro is now very popular with foreigners, particularly Germans. Head uphill on the path. After a sharp left turn, the *Associated* café is ahead on the left. Just before it, a signed path goes right then right towards the waterfall (the waterfall circular route described above exits here). Turn left just beyond the café and go downhill to rejoin the main road. Turn right and head to seaward along the road.

After passing the *Nelly* apartments and a dirt track on the left, join a path going diagonally up to the right in the same general direction as the road. This path runs along in front of houses, then rejoins the asphalt, but on the high side road into La Calera. Turn right and follow this road, going right at the fork. This road runs through the suburb of Las Orijamas, to a curving junction below *La Galeria*, where you should go right towards the sea, rather than back left and down with the main road. At the next junction, go left and down, then left and down again, to emerge by the main road.

Turn right. The road splits shortly afterwards, with the main road to Vueltas going on past the petrol station, roundabout and bridge, but go right into Carretera La Playa. There is no alternative to walking along this section of the narrow road, so you need to be careful of traffic. The road reaches the seafront, at the back of La Playa beach, near the small Ermita San Pedro. At the junction, the road left (unsurfaced at the time of writing) goes across the mouth of the bay, to La Puntilla and Vueltas, however you should go right. Turn left to go along in front of the La Playa shops, then turn right to go inland. Join the bigger road and continue onwards past large holiday complexes, to eventually reach the black sand beach of Playa del Inglés.

Return to La Playa and the Ermita San Pedro and then turn right along the seafront. The route goes along the back of the beach, passing the Hotel Gran Rey on the right. Continue on through La Puntilla, Charco del Conde and La Condesa to Vueltas.

18 Vueltas to Ermita de los Reyes to Las Pilas to Tequerguenche

An energetic, but not too long, route, up the eastern valley wall of Valle Gran Rey, then south along the ridge passing the once inhabited plateau of Las Pilas. There are spectacular views of the Valle Gran Rey valley, both from here, and from the southern tip of the ridge at Tequerguenche.

Follow **Walk 17** as far as the Ermita de los Reyes. At the junction just beyond the church, go to the right rather than steeply down to the left **(Walk 17)**. Swing through the back of a small, dammed, gully, then pass a *Parque Rural Valle Gran Rey* sign. A path zigzags up to the right immediately past the first house. Stay on the main path. About four

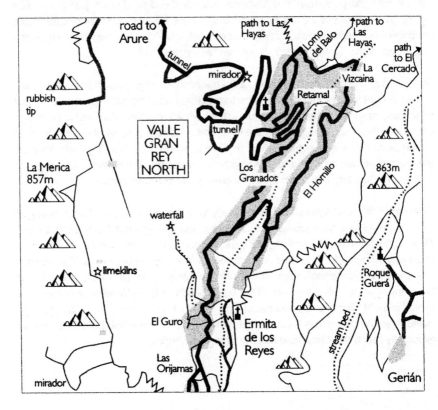

minutes beyond the church, turn off to the right, in the second smaller gully, immediately beside a couple of houses.

After about ten minutes uphill walking, you come to a viewpoint of the north valley. A couple of minutes more brings you to a junction where a path goes off left along the valley side, but you go to the right on the main path. Shortly afterwards another, smaller path goes off to the right – ignore this and continue on up. A steady uphill climb will bring you to the welcome pass, and view of the less-deep Argaga valley, in about 45 minutes from the bottom of the path. Turn right.

Go for fifteen minutes or so along a straightforward little cairned path, along the eastern, Argaga side of the ridge. Then swing around to the right over a red lava face, bringing you to a spectacular view of Playa and La Calera and the dip down to the final section of the headland. The path becomes slightly less clear as it rises to the broad plateau of Las Pilas, with its scattered ruins.
From the southeast corner of the plateau, faint paths run down to the further extremity of the ridge, at Tequerguenche, where high cliffs overlook Vueltas below and across to La Playa. This is about three quarters of an hour from the pass. Return to the pass by the same route.

You can then turn left and continue down into Valle Gran Rey, or alternatively – for a longer, but different return, stay on the path on the Argaga side of the ridge. This heads gradually down to the valley bottom, but look out for paved steps going up to the left. Take these steps back up to the ridge, and follow the path northeast along the Valle Gran Rey side. A long descent brings you down to join the surfaced road in the northern end of the Valle Gran Rey valley. Turn left to join the end of **Walk 13**, passing the bar *La Vizcaina*, and then down via the Ermita de los Reyes, to the coast.

19 Valle Gran Rey to Argaga to Gerián to Valle Gran Rey

Take plenty of water with you on this walk as the climb is a **strenuous** one, and can be very hot. The first section is an upward *route*, rather than a path, and involves some nontechnical climbing. It is not suitable for backpackers. Allow 5 hours for the return to Valle Gran Rey.

From the Vueltas part of Valle Gran Rey, follow the track that runs between Vueltas harbour and the high coastal cliffs, until you reach the next valley, the **Barranco de Argaga**. A concrete track goes up, at the mouth of the steep-sided valley, with various signs about privacy and dangerous dogs. If the gate is open you can go through, but soon you are led off the road by red marks which you should follow through the gorge bed, to the right of buildings and fenced areas.

At a black, rocky narrowing of the gorge, climb up past a small pool built into the gorge bed, to the stone terraces beyond and above. A badly eroded path zigzags up to the **right** of the terraces, then goes left across the top terrace. It continues, round to the right and leads into a section of the gorge with a gouged-out whirlpool below. Cross over the streambed and climb the eastern side of the gorge wall, on a very steep, slippery path marked with red blobs. *This is the start of the serious climbing, and there is more of it, so if you have doubts at this point, stop.* If continuing - from here, take a high level path along the eastern side of the gorge. This path drops suddenly as you come within sight of a grey rock-bed below.

Follow the gorge bed a short way, then climb a tall terrace wall on the right. Almost immediately afterwards, the path goes back to the right and up the cliff face. From here, follow the red markings. Avoid going too fast, particularly on apparently obvious sections, because you need to watch carefully for the next red mark. If you miss a mark, you may miss making a necessary turn and could end in an unsafe situation high above or below the correct route. As you go, try to memorize the way you have come. If you do then miss a mark, you can retrace your steps a little way, back to a previous mark, and try again, looking around carefully for the next one. The route through the Argaga is designed as a one-way path, going up only. It is *not* safe going down, and the red marks are not positioned for anyone going down.

Once you are at the end of the *climbing* section of the gorge, scramble up beside some old terraces and into the wider upper valley. The path runs along the right side of the valley, then rises by numerous zigzags up to the ridge on the right. This is a long ascent, and tiring on a hot day, particularly after your earlier exertions. Just before the top of the ridge, the path swings off to the left for a few minutes before popping up beside the houses of **Gerián** hamlet (700m/2295ft). The locals here are friendly, but their dogs can be noisy.

A dirt track comes into Gerián from Chipude and continues down to the southeast. Head uphill on this track, but in few minutes turn off left on a paved path above a house, back towards the rim of the Barranco de Argaga.

The path leads to the tiny Ermita of Nostre Señora de Guadalupe, at Roque de Guerá, a pleasant picnic spot. In the hillside immediately right of the church, there are two small, sunken caves. A path goes onwards along the barranco side, from the **level** of the ermita, but is in poor condition in places, so look for a path to the right of the church and go uphill. After a short distance, the path joins another and you go left. This path runs into the barranco and crosses the lower path. Follow the broader path down to cross the valley bed and then swing back up to the left. Pass a low cliff and ignore older paved steps going off up to the right. The path you are on ascends the ridge separating and overlooking Barranco de Argaga and Barranco del Valle Gran Rey.

On reaching the ridge, paths lead left (to Tequerguenche, overlooking Vueltas), right (to the upper Valle Gran Rey area), and onwards through a pass in the ridge. Take the onward route, which heads down into Barranco del Valle Gran Rey. There are long tedious sections in the first half of this descent, with one, unchanging view. The surface is loose and gritty in some of the steeper places, with rather less grip than is desirable. However the path eventually swings right and produces some new views.

As you near the lower parts of the valley, the path is apparently partly blocked by two slabs, raised on end, with a seemingly obvious path swinging back to the left. You should however go straight ahead, over the slabs. In a few minutes the path swings back down to the left, with a raised stone edge. Follow this path down. Lower down, the path passes a couple of houses, then turns immediately left onto the path to the church as in the last paragraph of **Walk 13**.

20 Gerián to La Matanza to Chipude

It would be possible to use this route as an alternative second half to **Walk 19**, to go to Chipude instead of back into Valle Gran Rey. A dirt track runs into Gerián from Chipude and continues down to the southeast, but the route here sticks to paths for much of the way. Allow about 1 hour.

Leave **Gerián**, initially heading uphill on the dirt track towards Chipude, but in a few minutes turn off left on a paved path above a house, towards the rim of the Barranco de Argaga. The path leads to the tiny Ermita of Nostre Señora de Guadalupe, at Roque de Guerá, a pleasant picnic spot. In the hillside immediately right of the church, there are two small, sunken caves. A path goes onwards along the barranco side, from the level of the ermita, but is in poor condition in places, so look for a path to the right of the church and go uphill. After a short distance, the path joins another and you go left. This path runs into the barranco and crosses the lower path. Go right here, along the valley side, rather than down into it. Stay with the path, swinging right into a narrow side-valley and then out again.

At **Degollada de la Matanza** just a narrow ridge of rock separates the Barranco de Argaga streambed from the huge Valle Gran Rey valley to the right. In geological time the Argaga will break through and become a tributary of the latter. A path (disrupted and impassable at the time of writing) goes off to the left of the ridge ahead, and down into Valle Gran Rey, but go to the right into the smaller valley, and then fork right to cross the stream. The path zigzags up the hillside, then joins a more level path. Ignore small side-paths, but go left on the level path. Follow this along the south side of the valley. Below the houses of **Chipude**, cross a dirt track and stay with the last section of path until it joins a short track to the main road. Go right and uphill on the road for the main church square at the top of the village.

2I Chipude to Fortaleza

Fortaleza (1241m/4070ft) is a flat-topped mountain, sacred to the Guanches, the pre-Spanish inhabitants of the Canary islands. Allow about 60-90 minutes to the top. Sections of the climb to the top can be unpleasant in strong wind.

Chipude (1060m/3475ft) is the highest large village on the island and, with the recently enlarged *Hotel Sonia*, is a well-positioned base for exploring the highland areas without the necessity of the initial climb from the main resorts. It is on the San Sebastián-Valle Gran Rey bus route and, in addition to the *Sonia* bar/restaurant, also has a small supermarket and several bars.

Coming out of **Chipude** in the direction of San Sebastián, the road curves to the left up towards the La Dama/main road junction. Before you get to a large house on the left, a wide cobbled path, with a sweet-chestnut tree to the left, goes up and over to the left. Follow this path up and over the ridge, across the asphalt main road (**Walk 22** goes left here) and down the other side of the ridge to join asphalt again. It is possible to do the same over the next ridge, but it is not so much of a shortcut.

Walk along from **Apartadero** village, past the petrol station, into **Pavon** village. The road swings down right below Fortaleza, but a broad paved path goes up to the left, beyond old Pavon. Follow the path up through the old village towards the saddle to the left of Fortaleza. Just past a little ruined house at the end of the village, a clear path goes off to the right. This then crosses a wider path and goes on upwards. Start up towards the large eucalyptus tree but, where the path forks, take the less conspicuous left-hand fork that goes nearer to the cliff over Erque. Both paths get to the same point but the left-hand one is perhaps better. White chalky soil marks the upper part of this path.

Rocky steps zigzag a couple of times, up the cliff, and after a while come to a flattish ledge to the right. At the end of this ledge is an unpleasantly steep-looking onward route up left. Move back a couple of metres, and look for the onward upward route, which is far easier, with placed stones higher up. Go up this section and emerge onto a side buttress of the main plateau. **Look back and memorize the route for your return**. Go off towards the main plateau over a short section, which is quite exposed if windy, but soon you are onto a better, rocky path. This runs just to the right of the connecting ridge and leads to the plateau. On the south side of the plateau is a trig point with views over the banana-growing village of La Dama, and the south coast. At the southeast corner a narrow ridge of rock leads to another buttress with further views east, and down to the spectacular cliffs of Fortaleza's eastern face.

22 Chipude to Garajonay to Contadero to Llanos de Crispin to Chipude

Allow 4 hours. The route includes Garajonay summit (1487m/4875ft), the highest point of the island. This altitude exceeds Ben Nevis by about 140m. At the end of the walk it is possible to go to nearby El Cercado village, instead of Chipude.

Start out as in **Walk 21**, but after the first cobbled path, turn left and follow the asphalt road towards San Sebastián for a couple of kilometres until you almost reach the *casa forestal*, forestry house, on the right. Here, take the dirt track up to the left, signed *Laguna Grande 4,5*. It soon swings back to the right and heads into the woodland. Ignore a later dirt track off to the left. Arrive at a 3-way junction marked *Laguna Grande* to the left, *Garajonay* straight on and *Las Tajoras & Chipude* the way you have come. A small footpath through the bushes to the left leads to *Chipude*. Continue on the Garajonay track past the chain. At the 3-way junction almost immediately afterwards, go right with the *Garajonay* sign. Follow the main track, ignoring any side-turns. There is one very steep section, followed by a turning off to the right that you should also ignore. After a further climb, ignore a signposted right turn to *Pajarito*.

Then, after a few minutes, turn right and up, at the last junction for Garajonay. This track leads to a small house, beyond which is the summit of **Garajonay**. A green spot opposite marks a path that leads downhill to a cross-paths where a path goes onwards, and then up again to a viewpoint. Go left at the cross-paths and down to the junction below Garajonay. Here turn right and follow the track down to the asphalt road. Turn left. The large carpark layby of **Alto de Contadero** is on your right, from where the El Cedro path leads off under the trees.

Stay with the asphalt for a while, then take a downward track on the left. There are large-leaved *Persea* trees, the wild Canary avocado, at the entrance. These are related to the true avocado, an American species, but the fat-stalked berries are small and not edible. The track swings back left then swings right again. Ignore the first and second tracks back to the left, but go to the right where it is signposted *La Laguna Grande 2.5km*. Left is signed to *Las Tajoras/Garajonay*. Continue and take the left, downward track where it is signed *La Laguna Grande 2.2km*.

The area around **Los Llanos de Crispin** has various dead trees including introduced pines and eucalyptus. The latter are commonly planted as ornamentals on the Canaries. On Madeira they have become so well established and abundant that they can prevent regeneration of the laurel forest. In order to prevent that situation occurring on Gomera, the eucalyptus growing in the National Park have been poisoned. Their ghostly white trunks and branches remain standing for a considerable while after death. It is fortunate that the Canarians do not have the bizarre Madeiran habit of enlivening virgin laurel forest by planting hydrangeas in it.

Emerge at the park boundary and a path off to the right is marked *Laguna Grande Sendera Forestal,* while the forest track goes on to El Cercado. Stay with the track. Just past a large flood barrier, turn left and down. The track goes below, and along in front of, the barrier, then across the valley and up the other side. At the high point of the track go to the left, underneath a water pipe. Keep on the descending main track, along the ridge.

Follow the track all the way if you want to go to El Cercado. From there, go right on the main road to Maria's café and you could then follow the second half of **Walk 13** *to Valle Gran Rey.*

For Chipude, where the track swings down and right, go instead onwards a short way to where a path crosses the ridge. Turn left down the path to the Chipude road, cross over and follow the path through the valley bottom to rejoin the asphalt road. Turn right into Chipude. After the second street lamp of Chipude, look down on the right and see the old, open-air laundry basins. Going on uphill, look for the bus-stop shelter on your left and take the steps up to its left. At the top of the steps join the track and go left uphill. A set of rough steps on the right will bring you out onto the asphalt top road by the supermarket. Buses will stop at the square above the church.

23 La Laguna Grande to El Cercado

La Laguna Grande is a high altitude depression in the central *Cumbre*, an open area in the laurel forest, at the junction of the Carretera Dorsal and the road up from the Visitors' Centre at Las Rosas. The area floods in wet seasons, and was used for gathering animals and, apparently, for witchcraft. There are car-parks, clean toilets, a child's play area and a good bar/restaurant serving traditional Gomeran food. The latter is very popular with coach parties and can be packed with day-trippers, but is very pleasant when less busy. In previous years it closed on Mondays.

There is a short, but interesting, marked path through the laurel forest from near the restaurant, with plenty of useful signs explaining various aspects of the geology, geography, botany and ecology. This circuit path has a good view of the Fortaleza de Cherelepín, a 1362m flat-topped mountain, rather less well known than the 120m lower but more spectacular Fortaleza near Chipude.

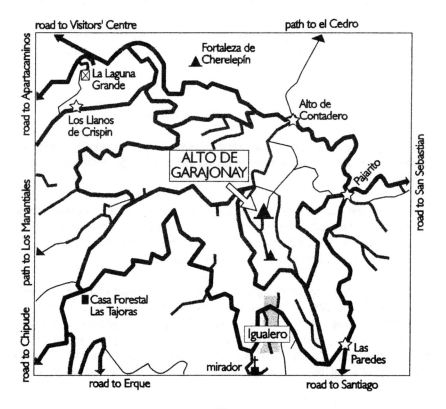

Walk 23 runs from La Laguna Grande, 1km downhill to join **Walk 22**. It then follows part of **Walk 22**, but to El Cercado. By going left, it would also be possible to return to La Laguna Grande, although one would need to walk along a kilometre of busy, pavement-less asphalt road top do so.

The start of the path is beyond the toilets, to the right of the **Laguna Grande** bar/restaurant. The initial descent is rocky, but then levels out. A junction at the bottom of the path, where it joins the Los Llanos de Crispin track in **Walk 22**, is signed back to La Laguna Grande, left to Alto de Garajonay 5.2km, and right to El Cercado 2.8km.

> For the circuit back to La Laguna Grande, go left on the track for about 1.2km, then left at the next 3-way junction. On reaching the asphalt road after about 0.8km, turn left and follow it to the Laguna Grande turn-off.

For El Cercado, turn right and emerge at the park boundary, then stay with the track. Just past a large flood barrier, turn left and down. The track goes below, and along in front of, the barrier, then across the valley and up the other side. At the high point of the track go to the left, underneath a water pipe. Keep on the descending main track, along the ridge. Near the end of the ridge it swings down to the right through the back of **El Cercado** village. At a 4-way junction of tracks, go left and down to the main road and bus-stop.

24 La Laguna Grande to Las Tajoras to Los Manantiales to Chipude

This walk goes from La Laguna Grande through wooded areas around the west side of Garajonay on the Las Tajoras forest road, and then to Chipude. Allow about 1 hour 50 minutes.

The start of the path is beyond the toilets, to the right of the **Laguna Grande** bar/restaurant. The initial descent is rocky, but then levels out. A junction at the bottom of the path, where it joins a dirt track, is signed back to La Laguna Grande, left to Alto de Garajonay 5.2km, and right to El Cercado 2.8km. Go left.

At the next junction, the set of signs indicate back to La Laguna Grande 2.5km/El Cercado 4.1km, off left to Carretera Dorsal 1.3km/Alto de Garajonay 3.2, and straight on to Alto de Garajonay 3.6km/Casa Forestal 3.0km. Go straight on, on the Casa Forestal track, and circle around the back of the valley before gradually climbing out along a ridge. Eventually you reach a high junction, with no signs at the time of writing. Right goes out along the ridge, but go left to swing down into the next valley. As you round the corner, Garajonay summit may be visible ahead. Immediately to the right of the summit are a small house and some masts. This should not be confused with the sister peak further to the right, with much larger masts.

At the next junction, signed Alto de Garajonay 2.3km to the left, and Casa Forestal 1km/ Chipude 2km to the right, ignore both signs. Look immediately to the right for a little footpath signed Chipude 1.8km. Turn right down this path and follow it for a short way through tree heathers and pines. It crosses a clearing and becomes a track, which curves down left and reaches another junction. Go right onto a fenced track. This runs high along the valley side, above numerous terraces, many of these abandoned and now collapsing. The track soon narrows to a wide stony path and continues towards the little settlement of **Los Manantiales** (the Springs). Look diagonally across the valley, to the opposite hillside beyond the village, and you should see your onward path. The asphalt road runs below you. Where it ends, go down and right, then left to join a level path below the main village houses. Go right, down very steep steps to the valley bottom, where a clear path leads up the other side. Where this path forks on the hillside, continue up, to the left.

Cross the ridge and **Chipude** is spread out in front of you. The path zigzags down the back of the little valley, then swings left along the back of the terraces. Join a steeply paved road and go down to the right. (*Coming up, for the reverse of the route, you should go left onto the path opposite some large green gates. Just beyond this turn-off, there is a long single-storey house on the left with (apparently) four windows.*) At a junction in Chipude, you should turn left to the phone box and emerge onto the main road, with the main church square on your right.

25 Pajarito to Garajonay to Pajarito

Pajarito is the high altitude (1380m) 3-way road junction, where the southern road from San Sebastián splits and goes left for Las Paredes, Santiago and the Chipude villages or right for La Laguna Grande and Vallehermoso. **Walk 25** is a circular route to the island's highest summit Garajonay and back to Pajarito. The summit is reached by clear footpaths and tracks and no scrambling or rock-climbing is necessary. In the winter half of the year, even with good weather below, heavy cloud can envelope the summit area above Pajarito, making an ascent not only unpleasantly cold and wet, but the views nonexistent. The weather can deteriorate rapidly, so extra warm and waterproof clothes are recommended, even on an initially fine day.

From **Pajarito** junction, between the northward and southwestward roads, a track is signed to Garajonay. Take this track and within a few moments turn right onto a stepped path leading off right for Garajonay. Follow this path up through scrub and woodland until you finally emerge onto the ridge at about 1460m altitude, east of the summit, and at a T-junction of paths. Go left, descending to cross another path, before the final ascent to arrive at the **Garajonay** summit area. Here at 1487m, there is an illustrated signboard with a panoramic photo naming various points around. From the summit descend past a little house, then join the downhill track to a junction signed back to Alto de Garajonay 0.5km, left to Chipude 4.5km, and right to Contadero 0.8km. Go left over the chain to join the Chipude track, but at the junction moments later, go left. Stay with this comparatively level track, which has good views of Fortaleza. Pass a skew cross-tracks to the south of the summit ridge (right here goes down to near the Las Paredes junction), and then the track curves left and starts to make a long descending loop back to **Pajarito**.

Pajarito to Olsen Hut

A recently constructed path parallels the main road from Pajarito down to the entrance of the Olsen Hut track **(Walk 14)**, and though a little rough in places is probably safer than walking down the road, particularly in misty weather. From the car-park at Pajarito, follow the track signed to *Los Roques* (- Agando, Ojila and Zarcita). The sign implies there is a path all the way to Los Roques, but at the time of writing, the path only went as far as described here, the rest of the way being on the main road.

After a short way on the track, join a signed path off left and follow this until it finally ends and rejoins the main road. Turn right, beside the road, then right again moments later onto the Olsen Hut dirt track.

26 Igualero to above Erque to Fortaleza

Igualero is a hamlet set in a loop of the main road in a small valley on the south side of Garajonay. To the east is the Las Paredes junction; to the west are a mirador and ermita. After a fire immediately beyond the mirador, it is possible to compare the dramatic difference between recovery of the Canary pine and introduced pine trees. The Canary pines, evolving on fiery volcanic islands, developed the ability to recover after being badly burned; the introduced European pines, by contrast, are now very dead. The path from Igualero follows the dramatic northern rim of the Erque caldera. It can be used as a continuation of **Walk 3**, from Las Paredes.

The path starts from the main road, just east of the paved access road into Igualero. It heads southwards along the valley side. At a fork go right. (Although if you go left, you will simply take a longer, more uphill, though attractive route. Turn right as you start to descend again on the far side of the ridge.) The path leads you out of the little Igualero valley, near the stream bed, and then descends, rather ambiguously, towards a clearer path coming in from the left. Go diagonally down to the right to join the new path.

The new path takes you northwest around the folds of hillside immediately above the rim of the huge Erque caldera. A more sheltered final descent brings you down to join a corner of the dirt road which leads to Erque and Erquito. Turn right onto the road which then swings left and uphill. At the next sharp bend in the road go off to the left on a path which soon leads down towards Fortaleza. Stay with the path to the main road in the hamlet of Pavon, and then go right, through Apartadero and towards Chipude (essentially, this is **Walk 21** in reverse).

27 Pavon to Erque to Erquito to El Drago to La Manteca to Magaña to Alajeró

This is a long walk with a number of ascents and descents. The initial descent into the Erque caldera can be initially vertiginous. **Walk 21** describes the route from Chipude to Pavon and the table mountain, Fortaleza. Not all Santiago-San Sebastián buses go via Alajeró.

The Chipude-La Dama road swings down to the west of Fortaleza, but a broad paved path goes up to the left, beyond old Pavon. Follow the path up around the south side of the old village, towards the saddle to the left of Fortaleza. There is a turn-off right for Fortaleza, but take the second turn-off right, a path that takes

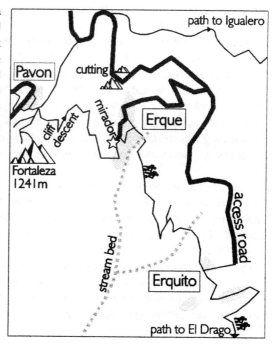

you to the rim (1110m/3640ft) of the Erque caldera and spectacular views. If you change your mind about going down the **400m** cliff in front, follow instructions*, to join the main walk at Erque.

(Alternative start, from Pavon to Erque, for anyone who does not wish to make the initial cliff descent to Erque. Return from the rim of the caldera to the main path up from Pavon and turn right. Follow it along, just outside the rim, until you join the dirt road down to Erque. Follow this road down as it loops through the top of the valley, through a cutting, and then above Erque village. A turning off right will bring you down to the Erque mirador at the end of this turning. Just before reaching the mirador, look for the path down left (right in the main text) to join the walk.)

Once on the rim of the caldera, just before furthest house on right, (which is that nearest to Fortaleza), look for the start of the steep zigzag path. From above, the path does not look promising, but it improves once you are on it. There are numerous, tall rocky steps on it, but it is reasonably clear. There are side-paths leading off it, used by goats, but you will find yourself being crowded uncomfortably by cacti and agaves if you accidentally venture onto one of these.

About ten minutes into the descent, you should be just above a path that runs in both directions along a rocky shelf. A short, black sub-shelf of rock, about 3m long, leads you down to the right and onto this more level path. Go along to the right a short distance, half a minute or so. The next section of the route can be a little hard to locate. There is an upright column of rock below and to your left, projecting from the cliff. Some smaller stones are wedged in beside it. These stones are the steps down. If you miss this point and go on, too far along the shelf, the path narrows uncomfortably. The rocky steps take you down about 6m, to join another path, where you go left.

At the end of this section of path, some more small rocky steps lead you down. The onward path then goes for a way to the left, before swinging back to the right. It starts to zigzag down a short ridge. Erque village, which has been in front of you, disappears from sight, hidden behind a tall, knife-edged fold of the caldera. Some 25 minutes into the descent, and still on the ridge, there is another short cliff descent, where you must work your way down a gully on step-like rocks. Once below this cliff, the slope is less extreme, and is covered with agave plants. The path heads down towards a large, distinct shrub several metres across, and particularly bright green in early spring. For much of second half the ridge descent, your route is towards the right of centre.

As the path approaches the stream bed there are scattered palm trees around. Look up to the left of the knife-edged ridge to see curiously shaped rock projections. At an ambiguous T-junction slightly before the stream bed, go to the right, then, within a few metres, back to the left. At the second junction, with mostly bare rock between you and the stream bed, you should go left and down. About 35 minutes from the rim the route arrives in the streambed (780m/2560ft).

Cross over, go diagonally to the right and join another path. Within a few minutes, this rounds a corner and a dark grey house, the first of **Erque**, comes into view. At a small rocky corner, before the houses, the path may appear to end, but continue around on the bare rocks, between two thin metal pipes, and the path reappears. Turn left immediately before the house, the Villa Garcia, and go up onto the rocky ridge. A steep zigzag path, then wooden-fenced steps, bring you up to a big paved mirador (800m/2625ft), reached in about five minutes from the stream bed. From here there is a view right down the valley, the Barranco de Erque.

Leave the mirador by the opposite entrance, heading inland along a dirt track. Beyond the first pylon, take a little path down to the right. Branch off left moments later, going down to join a level path along a terrace wall. Follow this towards a line of palm trees and swing left along a water channel. Where the water course swings off sharply up left, you should go right, over the rock, and join a broader path by a telegraph pole. Go down to the right. The path is vague in places, but continue descending, to the right of two buildings. The path should then be more obvious as it runs to the left of several more buildings. Pass a palm tree and go more steeply down to the left, on a path that is often stepped.

Go right, down towards a stream bed, and cross two water channels just above the stream. Then turn right along the stream bank. At a terrace where the stream swings to the right, go down a little shelf to the left to cross the stream on some faint stony steps.

Go up on the far bank. There is a big rocky corner on this side of the stream and you should edge your way round to the right of this. At this point it is overgrown with soggy vegetation, but around the corner the path becomes clear instantly. It heads off along the hillside, very quickly gaining height in relation to the bed of the stream. It swings left into a small, gully, by a power pole, and starts to zigzag upwards, about 15 minutes from the mirador and about one hour into the walk. The path in the gully is disrupted by a little flood-bed, but then zigzags off up to the right. After a few minutes, go around a large outcrop of volcanic sill, which from here can be seen to be the southern retaining wall of the Erque valley. A brisk climb, on a straightforward path, brings you up to above the altitude of the Erque mirador.

At a narrow ridge, there is a view of the scattered houses of Erquito. A track comes in from the left, on the hillside above, but your path goes on down to the left. Ignore a side-branch off to the left, up towards the track, and zigzag down into the first valley. Just before a little concrete bridge, ignore a smaller path off to the right.

Cross the bridge, over a very deeply-cut gully. Cross a dry streambed, with lots of litter, to arrive among the scattered and mostly empty houses of **Erquito** (700m/2295ft). Between a breeze block building and a white house with a tiled-roof, turn right and down, then left. At about eight minutes from the gully bridge, the path passes by a spring. Go up to the left on a paved path, by more houses, on a narrow ridge between two small stream valleys.

Continue steeply uphill on the paved path, above the houses, to reach a high ridge, above Erquito, on bare volcanic clinker. This is about one and a half hours into the walk. Looking ahead, you can probably see the walled onward path on the steep hillside. As you continue onwards, you will realize how many of the houses of Erquito you missed seeing earlier, while going through it, because of the very scattered nature of this settlement. A rocky zigzag takes you across to a junction, where the path goes on up left, and a very rough, disused track comes in from in front. Join the track.

> Purists may prefer to go up the higher, original path. It emerges at the crest of a rocky ridge, with a series of rocky terraces to the south, and becomes much less clear. Head to the right along the ridge, for some last views of Erquito back to the right. After a few moments along the ridge, the villages of Arguayoda and La Dama come into view on either side of the barranco. About ten minutes in, turn left on reaching the dirt track.

If you followed the track from the start, it leaves the dramatic barranco side and crosses a much gentler, terraced slope. The path mentioned above joins the track from the left.

As you round a corner at the end of the bowl of hillside, a junction with a bigger dirt road is just ahead. Down to the right is the small settlement of El Drago, en route to Arguayoda village. Immediately before this junction, turn right and down, onto a rough, walled path. At the rim of the barranco, this path swings back left and in the general direction of El Drago.

On reaching **El Drago** (660m/2 165ft), go past a junction, where another walled path goes back to the right towards the abandoned houses of El Topogache. Ignore a second path going right, by some houses. Go into the village, on a path. This path becomes concrete steps past the Villa Silvespe, then a concrete road, which joins the dirt road to Arguayoda about 2 hours 15 minutes into the walk.

If you wanted to detour to include Arguayoda, turn right after the Villa Silvespe and before the concrete road. See **Walk 28**.

Join the dirt road and head downhill. At a corner, where it swings back to the right, towards Arguayoda, a broad paved path goes off to the left. Go left here. The little conical hill of Alajeró is visible head, with a couple of masts, and a grove of large trees on the small rocky crest to the left of it. **La Manteca**, a tiny hamlet set in the cliffs of the Barranco de la Negra, comes into sight after a couple of minutes, about seven minutes from El Drago. Zigzag down through the settlement. At a junction, where left leads to houses built under the cliff, go down to the right and stay with the main path. There are spectacular views down into the barranco. After several wiggles of the path, below the last houses, it levels out a little and heads inland to the left, along the barranco side. About 15 minutes from El Drago, go right at a fork, where a more level path goes off to the left. Five minutes later, ignore a path joining yours from the right. Go left and moments later, ignore second path going back down to the right. Arrive at the stream bed a couple of minutes later, about three hours into the walk.

Go straight across and join the path up the other side. This goes up over the nose of the ridge, and then swings left inland along the side of the Barranco de Almagrero. In about seven minutes from the previous valley bottom, reach the next stream bed, where two cairns mark the crossing point onto an edged path opposite.

The path quickly starts to climb, zigzagging up. After about seven minutes up from the stream bed, continue to the right. Ignore a path going left around the barranco wall. A short while later, arrive on the ridge at the top of the barranco, at a junction with the Los Almácigos path. Here you go left, uphill. After about five minutes the path swings to the right, behind a row of houses, then diagonally up, without indication, across the bare rock surface. As you reach the end of the rock, Alajeró's Mt Calvario comes into view, and after going to the left of a palm tree, a short path takes you to join the end of an asphalt road.

Turn left onto the asphalt road and follow it up. Just beyond an isolated house on the right, at the top of a little valley, go to the right on a path. This leads towards the house, but turn off left just before the house, onto another walled path. This takes you into the next barranco, and passes to the right of the little cluster of houses of **Magaña** settlement. Continue into the top of the barranco, crossing the left-hand stream bed, then across to the right. Cross the little reservoir dam and then head uphill on a path to the left. In about eight minutes, and about three and a half hours into the walk, reach the top of the barranco. Join a dirt track here, and then another five minutes bring you to the first house of Alajeró. Go past the cemetery and then arrive above the main church.

28 El Drago to Arguayoda to La Rajita to La Dama

This route could be used as an alternative second half to **Walk 27** although it might be necessary to pre-arrange transport out of La Dama, at the end of the walk.

In **El Drago**, take the street alongside the Villa Silvespe. At the entrance to a green-fenced house, turn left onto a path beside the fence. In about 15 minutes, the path reaches the Arguayoda road which here, just above the village, is asphalt-surfaced. At the present time, only the section near the village is surfaced, and both ends of the asphalt revert to dirt road. Another five minutes on the path will bring you down into the main part of the village.

Once in **Arguayoda** (425m/1395ft), join the asphalt road and head towards the sea. Just before the end of the asphalt, turn left onto the original dirt track and follow this down towards the end of the ridge. Near the end, and just beyond where the track goes under power cables, are a yellow **H** and a cairn. These mark the path off left and down into the barranco. Follow the very long zigzags of this path, down towards the factory of **La Rajita**, which fills the mouth of the barranco.

The path ends at a little church. Go across in front of this, to the flood barrier wall, then left to the second telegraph pole. Here you should go over the wall, and down a stony bank into the river bed. Cross to the dirt track on the far side. Looking towards the sea, there is a bridge leading left to the factory gates, and a harbour area around to the right. The uphill path to La Dama starts from the hill side of the track, just left of some small buildings. Take this path up, initially to above the harbour area. At a junction, with a path ahead running under the cliff, turn back to the right and follow the path up to **La Dama** church.

La Dama to Arguayoda

It is possible to go to Arguayoda from La Dama by reversing the end of **Walk 28.** This is a shorter, but more strenuous alternative on a steep and often unclear cliff path. Once in Arguayoda, one could return to La Dama via La Rajita **(Walk 32)** or go on to La Manteca and Alajeró.

At the end of the long asphalt road down into **La Dama**, is a small church with a courtyard overlooking the deep Barranco de la Rajita. Stay with the now unsurfaced road as it curves around the church and makes its way down into the barranco. Twenty minutes down from the church, the dirt road swings right and back towards the sea and La Rajita. Moments later join a track going off to the left. Pass avocado and banana plantations and the village of Arguayoda comes into sight high up on the barranco wall to the right.

At a fenced enclosure where electricity pylons come in, go to the right of the gate, up a little concrete ramp and then down to the right. Cross over the streambed away from the ramp. Look for a cairn that marks the crossing, and for a little path opposite.

Follow this path along the right-hand side of the valley bed, for a couple of minutes only, not far beyond the end of the fence on the opposite side of the valley. Look for a point where the path forks, though not clearly, by a large cairn. The fork to the right goes up the barranco side, over a large rounded boulder set into the earth. The path goes up, diagonally, inland. It then zigzags, rather unclearly, up a black rocky area of the gully, before joining a steeper, clearer path with walled edges. The onward, upward path is in some places quite obvious, in many others you need to look around for stones that have been wedged into crevices or angles of the rock to create steps. There a few marker cairns.

Once near the village, the path heads off left and runs under a rock wall with natural openings and caves. It joins a much better, well-engineered path coming in from the left, inland. Turn right on this path and zigzag uphill to reach the village. In **Arguayoda**, join the asphalt road, and go right for La Rajita and the return to La Dama or left for El Drago or La Manteca. The turn off for La Manteca, described in **Walk 27**, is about 15-20 minutes up the road from Arguayoda. El Drago is about 5 minutes further.

29 Imada junction to dragon tree to Alajeró to Antoncojo to Playa de Santiago

Allow 5.5 hours. The bottom of the barranco at the dragon tree site is in shade in the early morning, and can be cold. You may need to wait a while to photograph the tree in sunshine. Not all Santiago-San Sebastián buses cover this route.

For the dragon tree, ask for *el Draco* and get off the bus near the Imada bus shelter situated at the start of the asphalt road to Imada. A new parking place and path for the dragon tree has been constructed using EU FEDER (Regional Fund) money. This path is quite roughly stone-surfaced and you may prefer to use the asphalt road to Agalán hamlet instead •.

> • *(Follow the asphalt road into Agalán hamlet. Immediately before the last buildings and the private road, a footpath goes off right, along the back of a house. It is marked with a signpost for the dragon tree, and white arrows and dots. Once past the houses, follow the clear track to the right for a short distance, until you reach the new path that descends to the left into the barranco.)* •

From the new parking place, a footpath starts down and zigzags to cross a dirt track. Right goes to a viewing point near a Canary pine, but before this point a walled path continues down left to the dragon tree itself.

When you reach the dragon tree, it is now securely surrounded and guarded by railings to prevent interference or the tree's possible escape. This venerable plant, probably several hundred years old, is the sole remaining wild Gomeran specimen of this species. There is an extensive program of replanting in parts of the island, including the Playas at Hermigua and Vallehermoso, and they are extensively cultivated in gardens. Most cultivated specimens on

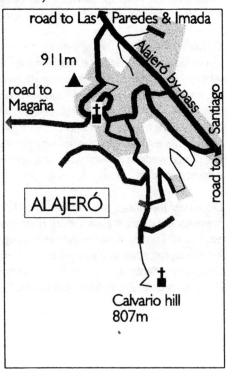

road to Las Paredes & Imada

Alajeró by-pass

911m

road to Magaña

road to Santiago

ALAJERÓ

Calvario hill
807m

the island are young and unbranched, and none are near the size of this wild plant. Dragon trees are found in Tenerife, Gran Canaria, La Palma, the Cape Verde Islands, and a few small wild plants survive on a remote cliff in Madeira. Until recently it was thought that they were confined to the Atlantic islands, but in the summer of 1996, several thousand trees were discovered growing in a remote area of the Moroccan Anti-Atlas mountains. The trees' dark red sap was prized in the Middle Ages as Dragon's Blood, and the timber was used for boat-building. Their slow growth and poor reproduction rate have made them very vulnerable.

Return from the dragon tree by the same route to near the viewing point, then turn right for Agalán. Turn left immediately before the first houses and then left onto the asphalt road. Beyond the corner after the last house, look for, and take, the small, descending, connecting path, going off right. This joins a broader, walled path, in front of some small vine terraces, where you go *right. If you miss the small path then, go further on the asphalt then turn right onto the top of the wider, walled and paved path.* Follow the partly walled footpath, which then wanders down to join the asphalt road just above the top entrance to Alajeró village. Take this right asphalt fork into **Alajeró** (836m/2740ft), near the sign for *Alajeró Casco* and follow it down to a mirador with seats. Take the steps down just to the *left* of the mirador, and the path emerges at a car-park. Go right, into the square, by the town hall, the *Ayuntamiento of Alajeró, Municipality of Europe.* Go round immediately to the left of the town hall to another, attractive large square, by the church, and enjoy the view. Turn left in front of the church, then turn right and down to join the road. At the corner, go to the left, passing the bar *La Alegria* on your left. If calling in, try to be there on the hour for the musical clock.

A possible detour here is to the Ermita of San Isidor, perched on the distinctly shaped hill of **Calvario** south of Alajeró. This hill is visible from many places, including the Los Cristianos to San Sebastián ferry if the weather is clear. Allow 1 hour extra. Turn right on the asphalt immediately past the football pitch. Continue on the dirt track, where the asphalt goes right, and go between new houses. Follow the track, then asphalt road, beyond the last houses to a fork and go left. Continue descending towards the north slope of Calvario, from where a stone paved walkway leads up to the little summit church (807m/2645ft). In the distance to the NNW is the isolated white Ermita of Nuestra Señora del Buen Paso. There are also views of flat-topped Fortaleza (NW), La Dama village (W), Quise hamlet below (WSW), and Santiago (SE). The pine trees at the *Jardín Tecina Hotel* are conspicuous. To the south is the original airport site at Las Petroleras, and left of this is the deep Barranco de Ereses. The island of Hierro may be visible. Return from Calvario, by the same route, to the sports pitch and turn right along the asphalt road.

Continue along the road through the village, passing the bar *Columba* on the right. The road then swings into a little valley and out to rejoin the main road. *Do not take an earlier steep asphalt road on the left that also connects with the main road, unless perhaps you want the official Alajeró bus stop and shelter that is at the top of it.*

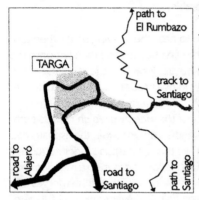

Turn right onto the main road, which bypasses the major part of the village. Stay with the road, in the direction of Santiago. After the last houses of Alajeró, and just before a left curve of the road through a low rock cutting, an asphalt road goes up to the left just as the bus stop shelter of Targa comes into view in the distance. Go with this road and shortly there is a view of Roque Agando. The mirador of Tajaque, and the occasional passing vehicle, can be seen high on the skyline to the left of Agando.

The road reaches **Targa** (750m/2460ft) village and winds down to a 3-way junction near the central bridge. Turn left on the dirt track along the left side of the valley, with the street lamps. Where the track bends left by an old building, your stony onward path descends on the right, immediately to the left of a circular threshing floor. Soon, at a fork of the path, go left. Out on the ridge, after a large cavity down to the right of the path and low rocky cliffs to the left, go right at a fork, towards the deep valley on your right. Look out for small cairns marking the path.

A zigzag descent goes down to the stream, where there is a lovely rock pool area, fine for a picnic lunch. Turn left along the bed, dodging low palm branches. Go to the left of a reservoir tank and the path resumes to the left of the stream. You will need to be cautious at a bend of the path, where a boulder narrows the path above the stream bed. A very short while later, cross the stream bed and follow a red-marked path *up* to the right. At a junction by a walled corner, take the left, lower path. Follow this path along the right-hand side of the valley, the Barranco de los Cocos, past a water chute and inscription. A view of a dam and **Antoncojo** village (520m/1705ft) appears.

Pass a small house on the right and join a dirt track. At the asphalt in the village, turn right and ignore promising green arrows pointing down left a few metres later. Stay with the asphalt, crossing a drain grid and head uphill a little. Turn left down a wide concrete and stone path, which soon swings right. Follow this path, almost level, for a while. There are views of Tenerife and Los Cristianos. At a fork by an electricity box go onwards and keep level with the lampposts. At a large junction go left and down slightly. Here there are yellow marks by the path.

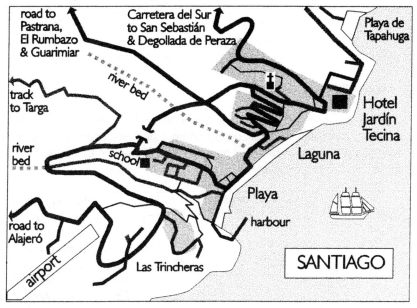

road to Pastrana, El Rumbazo & Guarimiar

Carretera del Sur to San Sebastián & Degollada de Peraza

Playa de Tapahuga

track to Targa

river bed

river bed

school

Laguna

Hotel Jardín Tecina

Playa

harbour

road to Alajeró

airport

Las Trincheras

SANTIAGO

The new, island airport's runway soon comes into view. The path runs downhill and towards a group of three houses with uniform brown roofs. Go to the right of the houses on a dirt-track, with a large dam and lake below on the left. A concrete-and-rock-covered water channel starts after the dam, alongside the track. Where the track swings round to the right, hop left over this water channel and join the path. This path swings right then left, then keeps to the left of two houses. It goes down eventually to join the main asphalt road, where you turn left and walk along it, passing the main entrance of the airport on your right.

Just before the embankment for the runway, a water chute comes in from the right. Painted yellow spots here, on a concrete crash-barrier on your left, mark steps down. Follow these to continue the path as the road swings away to the right. At the end of the path, join the dirt track entrance to a house and continue. Go left on a short path, but stay up with a paved section in front of a terraced white house, from where steps lead down to the main road. Cross the asphalt cautiously by the blind bend. Go right on the asphalt then almost immediately turn off left to the mirador and trig point of Las Trincheras, overlooking Santiago's Barranco de la Junta. After the mirador, continue with the path, turning left and down at the *Retevision* mast and building. Zigzag down to a junction with another path, and turn left. The wide path descends behind, then in front of, some houses. Turn right in front of the houses onto a small path that brings you out at the harbour end of Playa. Turn left for the square where the bus stops. *Alternatively stay with the wide path until it finally descends into the flood bed of the barranco, then turn right and follow the bed through into the square.*

30 Imada to Paredes

This route goes northwest from Imada village, to join the main Las Paredes-Alajeró road, about 2km below the Las Paredes junction. It starts from the small square by the phone box and bar near the inland end of **Imada** (850m/2790ft). Allow at least 30 minutes uphill to join the road.

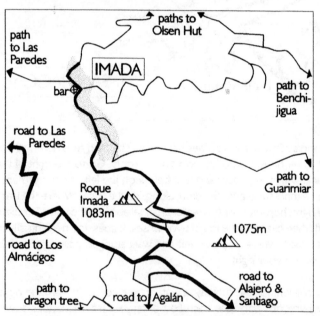

Go up the steep, asphalt just right of the bar. A short way up, turn off left onto some battered looking steps. About three minutes from the bar, a flat shelf of rock goes off left over a gully, but continue upwards on the main path. Cross a water channel in a few minutes later. Follow the rocky path and steps until at about 18 minutes into the walk you reach a ridge where a water pipe disappears over into a crevasse in front of you. Here you should turn up to the right, towards a palm tree. Turn left before the tree.

Emerge into a more level area, of gentle hills at about 1200m (3935ft) altitude. Pass between a small house and its fenced-in driveway, and go on uphill to join the asphalt road in about half an hour from the bar. Turn right, inland, on the road to reach the **Las Paredes** junction 1km above.

31 Pajarito to Imada

Allow 2.5 hours to Imada. If possible, get off the bus (not all Santiago-San Sebastián buses cover this route) at the entrance to the 'Olsen Hut' track. If not, get off at the big Pajarito junction a kilometre or so before. Follow the track from the back of the car park, signed to *Los Roques*. After a short way, join a signed path off left and follow this until it finally ends and rejoins the main road. Turn right, then right again moments later onto the 'Olsen Hut' dirt track.

From the road, the 'Olsen Hut' turning (1280m/4200ft) goes off to the right, southwards, and forks immediately. The left fork goes up to a radio mast. Take the right-hand fork, which cuts back sharply. Follow this track as it goes first down through woodland, then with wonderful views off to the left of Roque Agando and the Benchijigua valley. Ignore a track coming in from below left.

Shortly after a turn on the right, near some dead eucalyptus trees, the main track swings sharply back down to the right and can be seen continuing across the hillside. Here you should go straight ahead out onto the ridge, where your path soon swings off to the right. The edge is marked by a low wall. The path goes along the right-hand side of the ridge. The church on Calvario hill at Alajeró is in the far distance. Where the path splits, take a better fork going down to the right. From here a lower part of the path can be seen heading off near the valley bottom.

Take the left fork just above the rocky streambed, where a path goes off to the right and starts to climb some striated cliffs. Your path takes you towards the central ridge, stays on the left-hand side of the valley and brings you out above a much deeper valley. To the left is the Lomo del Azadoe ridge, with a reservoir and houses. Your path zigzags down to join another, better path, which you take as it goes right and up towards Imada village. Alternative **Walk 34** comes in from the left here.

You may wish to detour the short distance to the left onto the Azadoe ridge, for some wonderful views down into the Benchijigua valley and a good spot for a picnic lunch. On the high far side of this huge valley, the descending access track to Benchijigua and Lo del Gato villages can be seen, as well as an aqueducted water channel, and one of the new tunnels for the uncompleted Carretera del Sur.

Continue on the path to Imada, as it swings back onto a mini-terrace after the barranco bed. § See the last three paragraphs of **Walk 34** for the remaining details.

Imada to the Pajarito-Azadoe path

This route is a comparatively short connexion between Imada and the Pajarito-Azadoe-Imada path described in **Walk 31**, and could be used to extend **Walk 31** into a partly circular route. It starts from the small square by the phone box and bar near the inland end of **Imada** (850m/2790ft). Allow at least 15 minutes uphill.

Go up the steep, asphalt road just right of the bar. Ignore steps off left **(Walk 33)**. Stay with the rising asphalt, which swings right by a drainage chute then continues up less steeply. At the end of the asphalt, at a carpark mirador, your path starts, to the right of the last house. In a few minutes on the path, you reach the first stream bed. Look up left here for an interesting rock wall. Continue on the path. At a fork, about five minutes from the carpark, continue on the main path, where the other goes back left. About 12 minutes from the carpark, cross the ridge into the next valley where the path is much more level. Stay on the rim of the gorge until a crossing is possible, ignoring paths that lead off to the left. Cross the streambed and join the path on the far side in about 15 minutes from the carpark. Turn left and uphill, for **Pajarito/Olsen Hut (Walk 31** in reverse).

32 Imada to Guarimiar

This route follows a path through the narrow barranco below Imada down to the hamlet of Guarimiar, from where you can join the asphalt road to Santiago. **Walks 34** and **31** take you into Imada.

Imada village is a confusion of tiny steps, but you need to find the path immediately above the power tower, and to do this from the inland side of the tower. The tower itself is below the asphalt road and near the entrance (from Alajeró) end of the village.

Join the path and follow it onwards beyond the tower. It heads out on some brown rock, around the back of the head of the valley, and then forks. You should go left an down. Ignore a smaller branch off to right and follow the stony main path down the hillside, to the right of a gully bed. Ignore a path off left, where a metal pipe comes in.

The path swings off right and levels out for a stretch, below Roque Imada. It merges slowly with another path coming in from below left.

Pass a ruined house and then take the walled path down beyond the house. Once back on the earth surface, the path forks and you should take the downhill option to the left, which soon after is marked by a red paint blob. About 17 minutes down from the road, round a corner to a spectacular view of the Barranco de Guarimiar ahead. An obvious path goes off to the right but is walled off. You should look for a lower path. About 20 minutes into the walk, a narrower section starts. Follow the path down to eventually arrive in upper **Guarimiar** village. From here you can join the end of the asphalt road in lower Guarimiar, on the left-hand side of the valley. This road leads on eventually to Santiago.

33 Targa to El Rumbazo

Targa is a small village a short distance southeast of Alajeró. The walk goes down steeply into the Barranco de Guarimiar, and El Rumbazo hamlet, from where it is possible to walk along the asphalt road into Santiago. This route could be used as an alternative to part of **Walk 29.** Allow about 50 minutes to El Rumbazo.

An asphalt road runs into **Targa** from the main Alajeró-Santiago road. In the village it forks into two dirt tracks, the right-hand one running down the ridge towards Santiago. Start off down this track, passing the point where the path in **Walk 29** goes off down the valley to the right. Go along the track a short distance further, and a path goes off left towards a low point of the ridge. It is marked by a white and green sign for *Barranco Santiago/Guarimiar.*

Take this path and go through a little col, to a spectacular view out over the barranco. Follow the zigzag path down. After about 25 minutes, it splits and a level path goes off to the left and zigzags down towards the houses of Guarimiar. Right goes down towards **El Rumbazo.** Join the asphalt road below El Rumbazo and turn right towards Santiago.

34 Roque Agando to Benchijigua to Lomo del Azadoe to Imada to Alajeró

Roque Agando (1250m/4100ft) is Gomera's most famous *roque*, a huge upright volcanic plug astride the ridge between the Benchijigua and La Laja valleys. Your starting point is by the road, nearly 200m below the summit of Agando. Allow 6 hours to Alajeró. Not all Santiago-San Sebastián buses go via Alajeró.

Admire the view from miradors on *both* sides of the road first, then set off from immediately south of the memorial to a fire in Benchijigua in 1984. A signposted steep cobbled path, with steps, continues as a steeply descending stone and earth path. Follow it through a long tunnel of tall brooms, with pine litter on the ground, emerging occasionally to impressive views up the south face of Agando. The vegetation of this area suffered particularly badly in the long drought up to the winter of 95/96, but within a month of the first rain was already showing promising green shoots of recovery. You are not out in the open until you reach a concrete water channel 35-45 minutes from the start.

Once beyond the zigzag immediately below the water channel the path levels out and curves round the hillside to the right. Look back occasionally for good views of Agando. The rock and ermita of Benchijigua come into view and, below it to the left, some of the houses of the village. As you get near the village, with scattered eucalyptus trees around, the descent steepens and heads down the ridge in the direction of the ermita. Go right, under the trees, below the water channels, then on for a distance before turning left and down into **Benchijigua** (600m/1970ft), towards a long row of houses. Join two tracks coming in from the right and head round and up towards the Ermita of San Juan. (**Walk 35** goes from here and will take you downhill to Pastrana, for Santiago)

Return from the ermita to the foot of the church drive, and note several individually solar-powered *BP* lampposts installed just to illuminate this drive. Go to the first house on the left, a small bar which is sometimes open. Go left immediately before it, onto a chained track signed to Imada. At a fork in the track, go right. Cross a stream bed and then go right among the boulders beside the bed, to join a little path, and then go left where a path comes in from the stream bed to the right. People have been using the wrong route from just below here, and staying with the track. As a result the correct path is becoming overgrown in places. The ermita appears again, off to the left, and the spiky ridge of rock behind it. The path swings off right, passing a wall with some abandoned houses above on your right. It runs along and into a palm-filled gully, then climbs up to a rocky outcrop with a view down to the reservoir. Descend from the rocky area and join a better path coming in from the track to your left. The village of Lo del Gato (420m/1380ft) is below you.

After a small valley, climb up to some ruined buildings and an abandoned white house. Turn right here along the cairned path and soon there is a barbed wire fence to your right. These houses are at the base of a small cone of rock with a little pinnacle on the top. Once you get onto the hillside opposite the house, the path starts to rise, marked by occasional cairns. The stony path takes a long, zigzag climb up towards the top of the

Lomo del Azadoe ridge. Near the top, reach a T-junction at a slightly undercut natural rock wall.

*Our original walk route from here turned left, to El Cabezo and Santiago, but this path had stones placed across it in 1996 and we have not repeated it. We were told in early 1997 that it was still passable. See * at the end of the main walk for details.*

For Imada, from the T-junction on the Azadoe ridge, continue up to the right, to the top of the ridge (840m/2755ft), with good views into the barrancos of Benchijigua and Guarimiar, and of Imada village, and lovely picnic spots up among the folds of the rocky ridge.

Turn right just over the ridge and follow a clear path round towards Imada village. § **Walk 28** comes in from the right, just a few minutes along here. After crossing the bed of a small barranco, the path swings back onto a mini-terrace after the barranco bed. At the end of this terrace, climb up an area of smooth brown rock and the remains of the path on your right should then be obvious. Keep on going upwards to go above the ruined houses, to a little red-rock pass, and a view of curved basalt. At the next corner **Imada** (850m/2790ft) comes into view again. Follow the path, which winds down to a broad, brown-rock stream bed below the village. Cross the stream then turn right at the next junction of the path, to go up through the Imada terraces. Turn left at the top and emerge on the asphalt road near the phone kiosk and a small bar.

Follow the road out of the village, past the base of Roque Imada (1083m/3550ft). Once out of sight of the village, and just past an electricity pylon to the left of the road, a shortcut path leads you up, back to the right. Follow this path, rejoin the road and turn up it to the right. Very soon you should join another shortcut footpath to a higher section of the road. Stay with the asphalt up to and through the pass, with views beyond of a totally different landscape.

It is possible to go with the asphalt a few minutes to the main road, and catch the bus at the junction, but if there is time you may prefer to go on to Alajeró village. To do so, when immediately beyond the pass, turn off to the left on a rough dirt track. Follow this, and it becomes a path that leads along the hillside above the main Alajeró-Pajarito asphalt road, before finally joining the road a short distance before the beginning of **Alajeró** village. See **Walk 29** for details of the route from the top junction into the centre of the village. *To catch the bus from Alajeró, walk on left down the main road to the small white, orange-roofed bus shelter, to be certain of the bus stopping at your request.*

Lomo del Azadoe to El Cabezo to Santiago

Follow the main walk as far as the Lomo del Azadoe *, but note the comments there. The following description is from 19. *At the T-junction, go to the left along the line of the rock. You soon reach a widened corner where an apparently obvious path goes straight on, but look down to your left onto the orange rock and you will see where the correct lower path goes. Take this path and follow it along the ridge. After a time, the village of Pastrana comes into view down to the left. The path runs under cliffs and through a Heath Robinson orange plastic fence/gate. After the gate you will see the path beginning to descend a little - watch out for a zigzag loop of path that will save you scrambling down over the rocks.*

Initially the path begins to descend left towards Pastrana, but it quickly swings across the ridge and descends on the far side above El Cabezo village. It then returns to the Pastrana side. Follow it down and finally arrive again on the right-hand side of the ridge, heading down towards the asphalt road between Guarimiar and El Cabezo. Once down on the asphalt, turn left and follow the asphalt out of the valley towards Laguna de Santiago.

At a 4-way junction near Laguna, with the road-tunnel off to the right, turn left for the Jardín Tecina Hotel, or straight ahead and then right for Playa de Santiago. The bus stops outside the Tecina and at the square in Playa by the El Paso II Supermarket.

35 Benchijigua to Lo del Gato to Pastrana

This route could be an alternative second half for **Walk 34.** Allow about 90 minutes to Pastrana, then another hour to Playa de Santiago. Alternatively, it would be possible to follow the asphalt road from Santiago to Pastrana, take the direct path to Benchijigua and return via Lo del Gato - see the end of this walk for details.

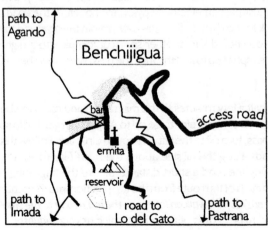

If coming into **Benchijigua** from Agando, turn left at the junction by the Benchijigua bar, and away from the Ermita. Follow

76

the dirt road, past three solar-powered lampposts, until just past the first house on the left. Take a well-marked path going off to the right. Lower down, under some eucalyptus trees, the path splits into a path off left and a gully straight on. Make sure you go left. Cross a streambed and continue onwards, then turn left before a large ruined house. The path zigzags down to join the Lo del Gato dirt road. You have a choice here. You could go up left to the next corner, and there go onto the path to Pastrana or, more interestingly, you can go right with the track to Lo del Gato and then on a path to Pastrana. Go right. Pass a dry, grey rock waterfall, then a larger side-barranco on the right with two levels of water-pipe and a dam behind. A further water channel can be seen on the hill far behind and above.

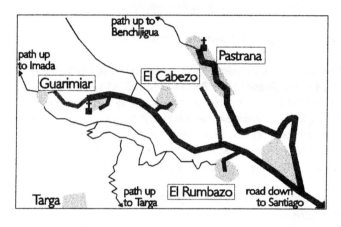

At the end of the track, in **Lo del Gato**, go down and left at the lamppost, then right on a narrow, stony, loose-surfaced path. At a fork, go to the house with a street-lamp on its corner, and along the passage between houses. Go left down steps, then right along in front of an old house. Go left and down again, and stay with the main descending path. Ignore confusing red blobs. Cat (*gato*) pictograms in various colours should help you find your way.

Cross the stream bed to the far side, and then swing right, up the path. There are several side-paths, but the main path runs between cacti, and to the right of a small house. Follow it around an outcrop, through a streambed, then uphill to join the other path. Go right, to Pastrana.

Stay with the path, crossing a stream bed and passing a small water-powered gofio mill, then rejoining the eastern side of the barranco. The path leads into **Pastrana**, from where the asphalt leads in about one hour, to Santiago.

Santiago to Pastrana to Benchijigua

Follow the asphalt road north from **Santiago** towards Pastrana, El Cabezo, El Rumbazo and Guarimiar. As you near this cluster of little villages, a fork off up to the right takes you to **Pastrana**, passing a bright red *Coca-Cola* machine. At the end of the asphalt, by a little Ermita, take the walled path that continues just to the left of centre. After crossing the stream-bed, pass a small water-powered gofio mill on the left. Continue up the stream bed, in the direction of a concrete water tank. Cairns and blue paint marks guide you by a black rock to a walled path on the right of the bed. Stay with this path, on the right-hand side of the valley, until you join a dirt road. Go left, down, for a few moments, then join a path going on up ahead to **Benchijigua** village.

36 Degollada de Peraza to Berruga to Contrera to Santiago

Allow 6 hours for the walk, since it includes crossings of three barrancos at the end. Buses will drop you off at the **Degollada de Peraza** (940m/3085ft) junction of the Carretera del Sur and the main San Sebastián road, but will also stop at the *Bar Peraza*, a couple of minutes along the road in the San Sebastián direction. Here you can have a pre-walk coffee or try the local donuts. From the windows you can see the rocky Berruga ridge, on which you will soon be walking. The *Jardín Tecina Hotel*, which you will be passing rather later in the day, is visible down near the sea.

'Degollada de Peraza' refers to the murder of the Spanish envoy, Count Peraza, who had his throat cut near here.

Cross the road from the bar and turn left along it in the direction of the junction of the Carretera del Sur. However, before you turn off down the new road, have a look from the mirador to the right, into the upper Barranco de Las Lajas and at the zigzag path leading down to the houses of La Laja.

Go down the new road. After 10-15 minutes walking, the new asphalt surface swings round to the right, quite sharply, through a new cutting that leaves a bit of the old asphalt road high and dry to the left. Go left up onto this old road and, where it bends back towards the new road, go ahead onto the ridge. As the ridge starts to climb, your path swings off to the right. The path is wide and goes along beside the first crest of the ridge, then around left behind a small group of houses. It curves east for a view of the *Bar Peraza*, and then heads out to the right side of the main Berruga ridge. The path leads along a cliff-face, swinging in and out of the curves of the mountainside, with spectacular views down into the Barranco de Chinguarime on the right. Behind, at the head of this barranco are the villages of Vegaipala to the far left and Jerduñe to the right.

At the end of the cliffs, follow the path as it swings to the left as the line of the ridge shifts leftwards. It crosses a flat, overhung area with recent rockfalls of large boulders. Steps had been cut out of the flat surface, but have now been partly covered by the falls. Not far beyond are some houses. Go right and down a little here, with the main path which runs alongside a red stone wall with rough terraces above and below. With the steep eastern cliffs of the Barranco de Chinguarime heading off right, the path climbs up through the terraces to a saddle with a rocky junction.

From here, clear walled paths go off left to Seima hamlet and right alongside the spine of the ridge. Turn right on this latter path towards Santiago. Soon you pass, on your left, an underground covered water tank. Upper Santiago suddenly comes into view, with the *Jardín Tecina Hotel* and its trees. To your left are Mt Teide on Tenerife, and, nearer, the old poles where the electricity wires descended into Seima. Alajeró's Calvario ermita appears on the far skyline on its distinctly shaped hill. Tejiade village is on the next ridge to your right.

The path continues down-ridge. At a big pile of rocks on the ridge to your left, the way swings down to the right, then left at a large cairn. A further cairn with splashes of white paint on it, on the right, marks the onward path, and there are more cairns en route. Note that many white paint marks in this area, and some very large cairns, are actually land boundary markers, not path indicators. Pass a little cluster of houses on your left and continue down a well-walled path until it emerges to the right of some more abandoned houses, the largest two-storeyed with a rickety wooden balcony. These are part of **Contrera** hamlet, and immediately in front of them is another junction for Seima hamlet, though this path junction can be overgrown after rain. Take the right-hand turn, which goes to the right of a broken wooden cross.

The path zigzags down over the rocks and then to the right of some tall palm trees. The other houses of Contrera can be seen down to your left. Cross over the stream bed to the right, and follow the path as it crosses back over to the left-hand side of the stream. (Do not continue to the right, despite cairns). Small cairns mark the correct path as you follow it down. Go up left onto a low ridge with views of abandoned houses of Contrera to the left, on the far side of a small gorge. Pass a subterranean, covered water tank on your right and a small cluster of houses on the left. Your path heads on down just to the left of the stream bed, following the cairns. The path forks by the stream bed and cairns mark the path off to the right, across the bed.

The path up left ends at a sheltered threshing floor and a couple of ruined houses.

The stream bed drops away and the path stays up high on the right rim, then goes round to the left of a disused house. White property marks are numerous here. The path wanders down the slope, goes under the power cables towards another house and a long straight section. It then turns right, parallel to the coast, after passing close to another small house. Soon there is a view of Tecina and the hillside above it. Beyond are the houses of Las Trincheras, and the new airport runway. Go a little further and look up to the right for a panorama of the hills behind, including Roque Agando in its saddle. You may seem nearly to be home to Santiago, but there are still three deep barrancos to cross.

Follow the path down into the Barranco de Chinguarime and cross the valley bottom to join the dirt track past the banana plantations. Go uphill for a short distance with the track and then turn right onto the stepped path, which goes up the next ridge. At the end of the path, go left of the building and emerge at a 3-way track junction, with a red dot marking the walled path down.

If you prefer to stay with the dirt track from Chinguarime, you should be aware that this is a private road and that after the next ridge the track descends and exits past a no entry sign, although it is constantly in use by pedestrians.

Either way, once down into the next barranco, Biquillo, you will join the dirt track coming in on your left from Playa del Medio beach. Turn right and cross the next ridge. On the descent from this ridge, a path down left shortcuts the dirt track into the Barranco de Tapahuga. After this you make your final ascent, to the Tecina ridge. On this ridge, turn right up an asphalt road between wire-fenced banana plantations, then turn left at the top and on to the entrance of the *Jardín Tecina Hotel*.

Past the hotel, turn left by the taxi and bus stop, and follow the looping road downhill towards Santiago proper. After a long, inland, descending straight, steps down on the left will cut off some of the following loops of asphalt in Laguna. Turn left back onto the road at the very bottom of the steps, and follow the now straight road through the banana plantations and then on to Playa, with its bars, restaurants, shops and pretty harbour. The bus picks up from the *Tecina* and the main square in Playa de Santiago.

37 Degollada de Peraza to Seima to Playa de El Cabrito to San Sebastian

Allow at least 4 hours. Buses will drop you off at the **Degollada de Peraza** (940m/3085ft) junction, where the semi-open Santiago Carretera del Sur meets the main San Sebastián road, but they will also stop at the *Bar Peraza*, a couple of minutes along the road in the San Sebastián direction. Here you can have a pre-walk coffee or try the local donuts. From the windows you can see the rocky Berruga ridge, on which you will soon be walking. The *Jardín Tecina Hotel*, in Santiago, is visible down near the sea. The walk takes you from the verdant cliffs of Berruga out into the dry terraces of Seima, an almost completely abandoned village. The route continues down to the sea at El Cabrito, then on along the coast to San Sebastián. Beyond Berruga, there is very little shade, and the walking can be very hot.

Cross the road from the bar and turn left along it in the direction of the junction of the Carretera del Sur. However, before you turn off left down the semi-open Santiago road, have a look from the mirador to the right, into the upper Barranco de Las Lajas and at the zigzag path leading down to the houses of La Laja **(Walk 39)**.

Walk down the Santiago road for 10-15 minutes. Where the new road swings round sharply to the right, through a new cutting, it leaves a section of the old asphalt road high and dry to the left. Go left up onto this old road and, where it bends back right towards the new road, go ahead onto the ridge. As the ridge starts to climb, your path swings off to the right of centre. The path is wide and goes along beside the first crest of the ridge, then around to the left and behind a small group of houses. There is a view left of the *Bar Peraza*, before the path heads out to the right of the main Berruga ridge. It leads along a cliff-face, swinging in and out of the curves of the mountainside, with spectacular views down into the Barranco de Chinguarime on the right. Behind, at the head of this barranco, are the small villages of Vegaipala to the left and Jerduñe to the right.

At the end of the cliffs, where the centre line of the ridge shifts leftwards, follow the path as it swings to the left. It crosses a flat, overhung area with recent rockfalls of large boulders. Steps had been cut out of the flat surface, but have now been partly covered by debris. Not far beyond are some abandoned houses, about an hour from the road. Go right here with the main path, which runs alongside a red stone wall with rough terraces above and below. Where the steep eastern cliffs of the Barranco de Chinguarime head off to the right, the path climbs up between terraces to a rocky junction.

From here, obvious walled paths go off left to Seima hamlet and right alongside the spine of the ridge towards Santiago (**Walk 36**). Go left, across the back of a terraced area, and then across a small ridge, near the poles which once carried electricity to Seima. At a fork in the path, go to the left, across the rocky hillside and behind more terraces. Cross a wall by a cairn, and follow a well-trodden path. Cross another little wall and the path takes you up onto a low ridge.

About 12 minutes walk from the rocky junction bring you to a spectacular view of the Barranco Juan de Vera, the Sombrero Ridge, the Barranco la Guancha beyond and then the Ayamosna ridge with the Carretera del Sur. Tenerife's Mt Teide is visible in the distance. Turn right and, within a few minutes, the terraces and scattered houses of Seima appear on the ridge below. At another rocky corner above the barranco turn right. Twenty minutes from the junction, you pass the first ruined houses of **Seima**. The paths are not very clear here, but you should go down and to the right of the next houses, where the path is obvious. Continue down a hillside zigzag, then at a fork go down and left. This path soon circles back to the right and to the main cluster of houses where there is the junction for Contrera. Straight on, between houses, is your route to Cabrito and San Sebastián, while right goes to Contrera (see the end of this walk) and Santiago.

A straightforward path runs out of Seima, mostly southward and seaward, out along the ridge. The ridge narrows, and some 15 minutes after the last houses of Seima, a clearly cairned path leads off and over into the deep barranco to the left.

> This alternative path ● zigzags down to the valley floor, crosses to the opposite side and then rises diagonally to the right, to join the Cabrito-San Sebastián path. It avoids the following long coastal detour around the *Finca el Cabrito* hotel complex.

For Cabrito, stay with the main path, to the right, along the narrowed ridge. This path descends further, out onto the ridge, and about 30 minutes from Seima reaches a small junction near the power pylons. Take the main path to the right and follow this out onto the red volcanic rock, to a little peak. There are views down left to the Cabrito area, while your path goes out onto the ridge in front. Your later onward path can be seen as a small zigzag on the far side of the barranco to your left. In about four minutes, you reach the start of the long descent to Cabrito.

Follow the initially straightforward path down, but at a false junction (right is just a drainage channel) swing back left, inland. A couple of minutes later, at a genuine junction, go right as marked by a yellow blob, towards the beach. The path drops to a junction by hotel buildings, where you should go right onto a semi-shaded path (almost the only shade on this walk after Berruga). This path joins a track coming in from the left, and you should follow the track out to the right, to the beach. Turn left along the beach front. In the past, when the area was owned as a private agricultural plantation rather than being run as a hotel, there was hostility to passers-by, but this no longer appears to be the case.

At the eastern end of the beach, about an hour from Seima, swing left onto a dirt track. Turn off right shortly afterwards, onto a rough track that goes past a rubbish dump and then along the outside of the hotel boundary wall. Little white concrete knobs with CP on them indicate private areas. After stepping under a barrier across the track, look out for a palm tree on the far bank of the river bed and for cairns marking the path to it. About seven minutes from the beach, climb a poorly surfaced zigzag path to reach a junction by a cairn in about ten minutes.

Here the path from the inland valley floor, and hence both the alternative path ● above and the path down from Sombrero (**Walk 38**), joins yours. Go to the right, over the ridge and down into the Barranco de Guancha in about 20 minutes from Cabrito beach. The onward path takes you down into the valley, and then follows it as it curves towards the sea, mostly staying to the left of the flood-bed. Pass a couple of little houses behind Guancha beach, then turn left and inland. In a few minutes you join a clear uphill path back to the right. This is very straightforward, with few bends, and you reach the top at just 15 minutes from the beach. Tenerife's Mt Teide comes into view.

In a further ten minutes, cross a dirt track as you descend into the next, smaller barranco, crossing its stream bed about three minutes later. From here it is the final stretch around the hillside below the statue of Christ and then San Sebastián comes into view. The path descends behind the power station, from where you can go right, to the seafront, or onwards to join the Carretera del Sur into San Sebastián.

Seima to Contrera

This is the connecting route between Seima and Contrera. Allow about 25 minutes. It is included, should you wish to switch from **Walk 37** back to **Walk 36**, or if you wished to go along the coastal route from San Sebastián to Seima to Contrera to Santiago. In the latter event, follow **Walk 37** in reverse as far as Seima, then the following, then the end of **Walk 33**.

Take the path to the right, southwestward, out of Seima. After a while, the green gardens of Tecina and its banana plantations come into view, then moments later the houses at Contrera with their palm trees. After crossing the next valley, the big Contrera house comes into view again. At a junction on the ridge, a yellow mark indicates a path off left, but you should go right towards the house. Moments later a gully appears, between you and the house. Follow the path down right, then, where it fades, follow the cairns, which take you towards a rock marked with a white blob and a painted **A47**. There are some small, walled-in fig-trees here. The path becomes clearer again, going uphill to the left. About 25 minutes from Seima, follow the path around the front of the largest Contrera house, to a junction by a smaller building below left of the house. Right goes uphill (eventually to Degollada de Peraza) and left, marked by a wooden signpost on a rocky peak, goes to Santiago. The rest of the houses of Contrera can be seen downhill towards the sea.

38 Carretera del Sur to Sombrero to Barranco Juan de Vera/El Cabrito

Sombrero is a distinctive volcanic outcrop on the ridge between the Barrancos la Guancha and Juan de Vera, visible from the main Carretera del Sur road out of San Sebastián. On this walk route there are barriers across the path, sometimes walls, sometimes of wood or agave stems. These are designed to contain cattle and can be stepped around. From the Barranco Juan de Vera, it is possible to go on left (north) to San Sebastián, or right (southeast) to Seima, Contrera and Santiago.

Start from the **Carretera del Sur** road, immediately above the Sombrero ridge, halfway between the Ayamosna turn-off and the *Bar Peraza*. This is opposite the very wide entrance track leading to an isolated house on the inland side of the road.

The path goes down past a few little shacks, where you should take care not to follow a more promising-looking path that heads off right towards the next ridge and a roque. Make sure you are on the path heading downridge directly towards Sombrero. Part way down, go round a small permanent cow-gate. As you near the first big rocky outcrop of the ridge, the Roque de Magro (679m/2225ft), there is a second gate. Go round to the right of the roque, and a third gate brings you into the little, semi-deserted settlement of **El Magro**. Occasional red paint blobs help guide you from here on.

A path back left from El Magro, on the other side of the roque comes in from Ayamosna and the Carretera del Sur. See the **alternative start** at the end of this walk.

Continue on downridge, towards **Sombrero** (657m/2135ft), arriving just above it in about 25 minutes from the start. Go to the right of it, then around another gate and onwards. Halfway between it and the next peak, there is a junction on orange rock. Cairns will guide you here, down the orange path, towards the next, more shapeless outcrop. As you near this outcrop rock, watch out for a turning back down to the right. This turn is cairned, but can be missed if your eyes are on the smaller path that heads directly towards the rock. Go right, and make a considerable descent to that side of the rock. Go under large, sheltering cliffs, then follow the path back onto the lower ridge. Pass between a little house and a solitary palm tree. The ridge itself runs between the deep Barranco la Guancha on the left and the deeper Barranco Juan de Vera on the right.

The path heads to the left of the next series of outcrops, climbs a little, then swings over the ridge at about 50 minutes into the walk. Follow the path and emerge some 3 minutes later onto a spectacular basalt platform on a jutting ridge, overlooking the bay of El Cabrito. The path runs along a narrow ridge, passing a twisted upright, basalt outcrop at about one hour into the walk. Past the outcrop, with Roque Garcia (351m/1150ft) up ahead, you should look out for cairns marking your path down to the right. A long and tedious series of zigzags bring you down towards the valley-bed.

After the descent, head seawards along the **Barranco Juan de Vera** and look out for a path up left, beyond Roque Garcia. Take this path, for San Sebastián, back up onto the ridge, to a large cairn and junction at about 130m (425ft). Left is for San Sebastián (see **Walk 37** for further details), right is for El Cabrito, Seima and Santiago.

> An **alternative start** for this walk would be to begin from the Ayamosna turn-off (a dirt track branching off northwards beside a house, to Ayamosna hamlet) of the Carretera del Sur. Opposite the dirt track, a path goes down into the barranco, descending diagonally to the right to the valley floor. It then climbs diagonally left to El Magro settlement, situated in the lee of the Roque del Magro outcrop.

39 Roque Agando to La Laja to Degollada de Peraza

This route descends from the main San Sebastián-Pajarito road deep into the Barranco de las Lajas, and then rises to rejoin the road at the Degollada de Peraza. It involves a descent of 450m followed by an ascent of 400m. Allow about 2 hours.

The start of this path is just below **Roque Agando**, going off left from the main road towards San Sebastián, and is clearly signed. Follow the path, down to a disused forestry house on a ridge. The path continues down to the right, from immediately before the house, but is partly blocked here by a fallen tree. You can go to the end of the house terrace and then down right, bypassing the tree, and rejoining the main path. Further down, in the valley, the path passes a rock and wire flood-barrier.

The route is straightforward from here. The path nears the valley bottom, above the houses of the inland end of **La Laja**, and swings to the right. A small path goes down left to the houses, but stay on the more level path and then go right at the next junction. This brings you around the back of a small bowl of hillside and up to join a second, steeper path up from central La Laja.

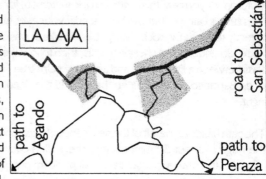

The asphalt road from La Laja runs eastwards along the valley floor, eventually to San Sebastián, via the settlements of Chejelipes, Lomito Fragos y Honduras, El Atajo, El Jurado and San Antonio.

Stay with the ascending path, which climbs the north-facing wall of the barranco. Ignore two branches off to the left, and finally zigzag up to the **Degollada de Peraza** mirador (940m/3085ft). The *Bar Peraza* is down to the left, Roque Agando is up to the right.

40 Roque Agando to Degollada de Peraza to Ayamosna to San Sebastián

Allow 5 hours for this walk, which follows a high ridge down to the island's capital, with spectacular views en route. From the miradors (1060ft/3475ft) at **Roque Agando**, head back along the main road towards San Sebastián. The road goes through a low cutting with, on the left-hand side, two vertical bands of intrusive rock. Immediately before a much deeper cutting, a path goes off up to the left, opposite the falling-rock road-sign. A yellow mark on the rock confirms it. Some of the vegetation around the path has been cut down to create a firebreak, but continue up the clearing to find the onward path. This sheltered path leads you up and over a summit, then opens out to a wider track to the Ermita de las Nieves. From the ermita, follow the dirt track down until just before it swings back down to the right to join the main road. Here a reddish earth track comes off on the left, climbing slightly. Follow this track to the right of a little pink house, with a mirador down to La Laja and upvalley. Stay with the track down from the house, and go to the right of an orange-yellow outcrop of rock into a water-worn gully with a fence on the right-hand side. Join an old, paved cobble path. Finally, a more recent path descends to the road, doing so very steeply at the end.

Head left along the main road, past the **Degollada de Peraza** mirador, to the *Bar Peraza* on your right. After a small, low cutting a few minutes along the road beyond the bar – not up the track immediately beyond the bar – there on your left are some fenced-off white concrete buildings. Just beyond them your track starts up, to run not far above, and parallel with, the main road. It is a clear, wide brown track lined on the

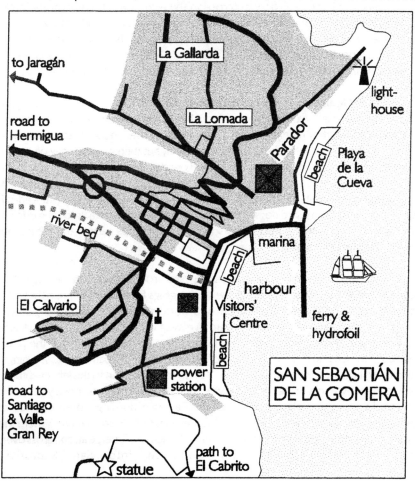

right by *Agave* plants. Do not take the path up to the summit (Tagamiche 979m/3210ft) on the left. Below the summit aerials the path loops back to the right and heads down towards the road, however, you should join the original track that zigzags off left from this path. There is a red mark on a stone. The onward path is visible down on your left, under a clump of thick-trunked palm-trees. By the time you are level with the road, you are heading off somewhat to the left of Mt Teide on Tenerife and towards a little clump of palm-trees.

At the next low ridge, rocks on top of a big boulder mark the path, which then zigzags down into the next valley. Past a closed-up house, the well-engineered path climbs up to the right-hand side of a rocky outcrop on the next ridge. It runs over the rock surface, with a sea of prickly pear cacti on the right-hand side, heading towards the next little rocky summit. A paved, walled path goes off to the right by an electricity pole, but ignore this turning and go left, ascending slightly. The distinctive Sombrero peak (657m/2155ft) can be seen on the far side of the valley to the right.

The hamlet of **Ayamosna** (685m/2245ft) is tucked against rocks on either side of a gap in the ridge to the left. A dirt track appears on the left and runs parallel to your sunken, walled path, until they merge just past a newly-built house. The dirt track runs down to a T-junction. Turn left here towards Ayamosna, but then go diagonally off to the right on the old path with its blue paint mark. Towards the end of the ridge your path swings to the left and starts to descend fairly steeply, with views of San Sebastián and the harbour. A disrupted section of path runs down the left-hand side of a fenced-off area of buildings with guard dogs. It continues down and joins a track coming in from the right. Go left with the track. Very soon this track loops back to the left but an onward footpath cuts off the corner.

Rejoin and follow the track onwards, passing a red-roofed house on the ridge. At a corner above a semi-ruined house, the track zigzags back down to the right and a small track goes on, but go between them on a shortcutting chalky path heading down. Rejoin and turn left with the track towards a row of white houses, which are clearly visible near the skyline *from* San Sebastián. However, just before them take the wide, walled path descending in the direction of San Sebastián. This path zigzags seemingly endlessly, at first on the top of the ridge, then to the right, then to the left. Eventually you come down to a white concrete water tank. Beyond the tank, once you are on dirt tracks, go left and inland around the end of a row of buildings. Join the asphalt of *Avenida de las Galanas* and head down, then left into *Calle Fuerteventura*. Where the asphalt ends, turn right and down into *Cañada del Herrero*. Emerge at, and cross over, the main road bridge and walk on into San Sebastián.

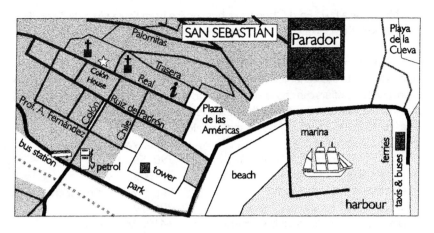

-----oooOooo-----

Appendix I   some relevant Spanish

alto	high, high place	mirador	viewpoint
autobús	bus	montaña	mountain
barranco	gorge, deep valley	parada	bus stop
bosque	wood, forest	pista	track, trail
camino	road, way, track	playa	beach, flat area
cañada	gully, ravine, cattle-track	privado	private
carretera	main road	raso	flat, level
casa	house, building	risco	cliff
caserío	hamlet, country house	roca	rock
ermita	church	roque	rook (chess), a large rock
guagua	bus	tower	
laguna	lake, gap	senda, sendero	path, track
llano	plain	s/n	without a number
lomo	ridge		

Appendix 2   Travel – Ferries and Buses

FERRIES AND HYDROFOILS connect San Sebastián de la Gomera with Los Cristianos on Tenerife. Los Cristianos port is approximately 20km from the Tenerife South airport. There are occasional TITSA buses between the airport and the port. It is also possible to use a taxi. Fred Olsen run a bus service from Santa Cruz de Tenerife to connect with their ferries.

Fred Olsen/Gomera Ferry and Trasarmas/GomeraJet have recently introduced express ferries to the Tenerife-Gomera route. These two companies are competitive, so prices/special offers can change from week to week, and there are discounts for the over-60s, students and children. There are less frequent connections between San Sebastián and the islands of Hierro and La Palma.

Fred Olsen/Gomera Ferry	http://www.fredolsen.es
•Harbour, Los Cristianos (Tenerife)	790556
•Paseo de Fred Olsen s/n, San Sebastián	871007
Trasmediterránea/Trasarmas	http://www.trasmediterranea.es
•Harbour, Los Cristianos	796179
•Harbour, San Sebastián de la Gomera	141969/fax 871324
•Valle Gran Rey	805968/fax 805968
•Los Cristianos (Tenerife)	753867/795463/fax 796179

PUBLIC BUS LINES on Gomera start and end at the port in San Sebastián. They are synchronized to some extent with the ferry times, and can leave San Sebastián port early, if they have all the incoming ferry passengers. Journey time from one end of the line to the other is approximately 60-120 minutes, depending on line, traffic and weather. The best way to find out the bus times for all three lines is to look at a bus windscreen. Usually the driver has the routes and times displayed here, and will give you a small printed slip of paper with these on, if asked. Buses can be very full leaving Valle Gran Rey in the morning, and you may not be able to get on. Be sure to signal clearly with your arm if you want buses to stop for you en route!

Line 1	**San Sebastián**-Degollada de Peraza-Roque Agando-Pajarito-Las Paredes-Chipude-El Cercado-for Las Hayas-Apartacaminos-Arure-**Valle Gran Rey**
Line 2	**San Sebastián**-Degollada de Peraza-Carretera del Sur-Tecina-Playa de **Santiago**-Alajeró one morning bus usually goes Tecina-Playa de **Santiago**-Alajeró-Las Paredes-Pajarito-Roque Agando-Degollada de Peraza-**San Sebastián**
Line 3	**San Sebastián**-Hermigua-Playa de Hermigua-Agulo-Las Rosas-**Vallehermoso**

Taxis can be used, but establish a price before departure. If you have arranged to be collected, try to have with you the driver's name, phone number and taxi number, *in* *case* you need to change your plans (though there may not be a telephone en route!). There are many others, other than those listed below:

Alojera	800259
Chipude	804158
Hermigua – Playa Sta Catalina	[Ramon] 880700, mobile 608.028741
Santiago	[Ramon] 895002
Santiago	[Sarada] 895022
Valle Gran Rey	[Carlos] 805650, mobile 608 029577
Valle Gran Rey – taxi-stand	805058

La Gomera Airport (QGZ) did not have scheduled services at the time of writing. Services are planned by NAYSA (tel: 759691/873024) from Tenerife South and La Palma, by Binter (tel: 635788) from Tenerife North and Gran Canaria, and by Air Atlantic (tel: 928-261683) from Gran Canaria.

Appendix 3   Useful information

Telephone code 0034922 from UK, 0922 from Spain or Canaries other than Tenerife.

Postcodes: 38000 San Sebastián de la Gomera, 38810 Santiago, 38820 Hermigua, 38830 Agulo, 38840 Vallehermoso, 38870 Valle Gran Rey

GARAJONAY NATIONAL PARK

Visitors' Centre, Juego de Bolas, Las Rosas	800993
ICONA, Carretera General del Sur 20, San Sebastián	870105

TOURIST OFFICES

C.I.T. Rural, PO Box 1, Hermigua	144101/fax 144101
Calle Real 4, San Sebastián de la Gomera	141512/870281/fax 140151
Avda. Marítima s/n, Playa de Santiago	895650/fax 895651
Calle Lepanto s/n, La Playa, Valle Gran Rey	805458/fax 805458
C.I.T. Rural, Plaza de la Constitución 1, Vallehermoso	800000/800075

• website: http://www.gomera-island.com
• e-mail: turismo@gomera-island.com

AECAN/Rural Lodgings in Canaries (Tenerife, La Gomera, El Hierro, La Palma)
• Tenerife office   240816/fax 244003

HIRE CARS are reasonably priced and available in San Sebastián, Hermigua, Santiago and Valle Gran Rey. When driving be aware that there may be fallen rocks in the road, particularly during wet weather and more so on the north coast between Agulo and Chorros de Epina. Be aware on corners that oncoming traffic may be on your side of the road as they avoid a fallen rock. Heavy rain or strong winds can also bring down the occasional laurel tree.

Central San Sebastián has a **permit parking system**, but there are usually plenty of unrestricted spaces alongside the main river bed. Do not leave valuables in sight, as cars do get broken into, particularly in remote forest parking spaces. There are **petrol stations** in the main towns, but the only one in the centre of the island is at Apartadero, between Chipude and Fortaleza.

CAR-HIRE – SAN SEBASTIÁN

Autos Garajonay,	871362
La Rueda car-hire, Calle del Real 19, San Sebastián	870709/fax 870142
Rent a Car Piñero	
• Avda. José Aguiar 14, San Sebastián	141048/870055/fax 141390,
• Estación Marítima	870148
• Calle Real	870888

CAR-HIRE – SANTIAGO

Rent a Car Piñero	
• Paseo Marítimo, Playa de Santiago	895281
• Hotel Jardín Tecina	895180

CARHIRE – VALLE GRAN REY

La Rueda car-hire, Calle La Playa, Valle Gran Rey	805197/805517
Rent a Car Piñero	
• Ctra. Vueltas 94, Valle Gran Rey	805397
• Playa de la Calera, Valle Gran Rey	805227
• Ctra. La Puntilla, Valle Gran Rey	805686

ACCOMMODATION

San Sebastián has accommodation, but the first buses do not depart until late morning, so are not good for starting long walks. By staying towards the other end of bus lines you can use the early morning services, towards San Sebastián, for gaining altitude and starting walks.

Please note that listings in tourist office literature are often by council districts, not by adjacent areas. Under this system, rather confusingly, the eastern half of Santiago

(Laguna and Tecina) appear under San Sebastián, and the western half of Santiago (Playa) appears under Alajeró. Similarly, due to district boundaries, Argaga, which is next door to Valle Gran Rey, is listed under Vallehermoso on the north side of the island. However, in the following text, all Santiago listings are together, and Argaga appears with Valle Gran Rey.

In the listings, pensions and hotels are given their official star-rating; apartments are 3rd class unless otherwise stated. Apartment units with 10+ apartments are marked with a §.

AGULO HOTEL/APARTMENTS

Hotel Casa de los Pérez	146122 (after 20.00: 880901)/fax 146151
Bajip Apts	880929

ALOJERA APARTMENTS

Mesa Apts.	800165
Ossorio Apts./bar-restaurant, *Alojera, Vallehermoso*	800334
Playa de Alojera Apts	800217/800703
Vega Hernandez Apts	800337

CHIPUDE HOTEL

Hotel Sonia, *La Plaza*	804158

EL CABRITO HOTEL

Hotel Finca El Cabrito
    (in Germany: tel: 02255 950095/fax: 950097/e-mail: info@neuewege.com)

HERMIGUA PENSIONS/HOTELS

Hotel Ibo Alfaro, *Ibo Alfaro*	880168 (after 20:00: 880901)/fax146151
La Punta Pensión, *Carretera General 271*	880253

HERMIGUA APARTMENTS

La Casa Creativa	881023/fax 144057
Casa Margot Apts., *Los Gomeros*	870978
Playa Apts., *Playa Santa Catalina*	144064, fax 880152
Santa Catalina Apts. (+ Taxi), *Playa Sta Catalina*	880700, mobile 608.028741
Los Telares Apts.§, *El Convento*	880781/880901/fax 144107

SAN SEBASTIÁN PENSIONS/HOTELS

Pensión Colombina*, *Ruiz de Padrón 81*	871257
Pensión Colon**, *Calle Real 59*	870235
Hotel Garajonay **, *Ruiz de Padrón 17*	870550/fax 870554
Pensión Gomera*, *Calle Real 33*	870417
Pensión Hesperides**, *Ruiz de Padrón 42*	871305
Hostal El Pajar*, *Calle Real 23*	870207

Parador Nacional****, *Cerro la Horca* 871100/fax 871116
Hotel Villa Gomera**, *Ruiz de Padrón 68* 870020

SAN SEBASTIÁN APARTMENTS

Arteaga, *Prof. Armas Fernández 13* 141213
Bernabe Apts., *Prof. Armas Fernández 16* 870503
Canarias Apts., *Ruiz de Padrón 3* 141453
Casa Roland Apts. (2nd), *La Costa* 870104
Cataysa Apts., *Pista de las Palomitas 1* 870396
Chijere Apts., *Llano la Villa* 871113
Garcia Apts., *Calle Real 27* 870652
Guadalupe Apts., *Pista de las Palomitas 8* 870842
Mari y Teide Apts., *Carretera del Faro* 870104
Miramar Apartments, *Orilla del Llano (Llano la Villa) 3* 870448
Mora Apts., *Calle Trasera 36* 870442
Orquidea Apts. § (2nd), *Avenida de Colon 22* 871488
Pepita Apts., *Callejon de Minela 2* 871376
Quintero Apts. § (2nd), *Plaza de las Americas 6* 141744
San Sebastián Apts.§, *Calle Real 20* 871354/fax141475

SANTIAGO PENSIÓN/HOTELS

El Carmen Pensión*, *Playa de Santiago* 895028
Casanova Pensión* & Apts., *Avenida Maritima, Playa de Santiago* 895002
La Gaviota Pensión**, *Playa de Santiago* 895135
Hotel Jardín Tecina****, *Santiago* 895050/fax895188

SANTIAGO APARTMENTS

El Balcón de Santa Ana § (available to investors of Holiday Property Bond. UK tel: 01638 660066/fax:660213/e-mail: info@hpb.co.uk) – due to open end 2000
Bellavista Apts., *Laguna* 895208
Bertin Apts., *Laguna* 895250
Casanova Apts. & Pensión, *Playa* 895002
Lourdes Apts., *Playa* 285727
Mari Carmen Apts., *Calle Santa Ana 37, Laguna* 895249
Negrin Apts., *Laguna* 895282
Eligio Negrin Apts., *Las Trincheras* 895138
Negrin 3 Apts., *Barranco* 895282
Nemtru Apts., *Laguna* 895138
Noda Apts., *Laguna* 895087
Padilla Apts., *Las Trincheras* 895057
Parada Apts., *Cueva Honda, Playa* 895062
Playa Apts/bar-restaurant, *Avenida Maritima, Playa* 895147/895120

Sebas Apts., *Tecina*	895078
Tapahuga Apts.§ (1st), *Avenida Marítima, Playa*	895159/fax 895127
Las Trincheras Apts., *Las Trincheras*	895166
Vera Apts., *Avenida Maritima, Playa*	895146

VALLE GRAN REY HOTELS/PENSIONS

Hotel Gran Rey, *La Puntilla*	805859/fax 805651

• website: http://www.hotel-granrey.com
• e-mail: webmaster@hotel-granrey.com

Pensión Candelaria*, *Vueltas*	805402
Pensión Las Jornadas*, *Playa de la Calera*	805047
Pensión Parada*, *El Caidero*	805052
Pensión Playamar**, *La Playa*	805672
Pensión Ramon*, *La Calera*	805404
Pensión Las Vueltas*, *Vueltas*	805216
Pensión Villa Aurora, *Borbolán*	
Pensión Playa Argayall*, *Playa de Argaga*	805312

Since there are so many apartments in Valle Gran Rey, these are listed by area

VALLE GRAN REY - LA CALERA APARTMENTS

Armas Apts. (805187)... Bella Vista Apts. (805151)... Casa Uli Apts. (805057)... Concha Apts. (805007)... El Contero Apts. (805056)... Chinea Apts. (805232)... El Chorro Apts. (805291)... Dominguez-Megina Apts. (805030)... Dominguez-Roldan Apts. (805181)... Eva Apts. (805145)... La Galeria Apts. (805477/fax 805366)... El Garage Apts. (805129)... Glorimar Apts. (805032)... Lancon Apts. (805171)... Mesa Apts. (805699)... El Mirador Apts. (805046)... Nudali Apts. (805256)... Orone Apts. (805283)... Puesta del Sol Apts. (s/n)... Rivas Apts. (805068)

VALLE GRAN REY - BORBALÁN APARTMENTS

Alpina Apts. (805128)... Azahares Apts. (805128)... Borbalán Apts. (805021)... Canario Apts. (805139)... Iballa Apts. (805152)... Palomera 2 Apts. (805129)... El Platanal Apts. (805124)

VALLE GRAN REY - LOS GRANADOS APARTMENTS

Lucia Apts. (805407)...

VALLE GRAN REY - El GURO APARTMENTS

Nelly Apts., *Cañada la Rosa* (805084)...

VALLE GRAN REY - LAS ORIJAMAS (Upper La Calera) APARTMENTS

Ana Rosa Apts. (805226)... Conchita Apts. (805452)... Damas Apts. (805288)... Ernesto Apts. (805168)... Gran Rey Apts. (805039)... Lili Apts. (s/n)... Los Naranjos Apts. (805168)... Nina Apts. (805276)... Veronica Apts. (805243)

VALLE GRAN REY - LA PLAYA/CARRETERA PLAYA DEL INGLES APARTMENTS
Amalia Apts. (571129)... Apts., Amalia Negrin Dorta/Jesus Medina Morales (805626)... Balcon Canario Apts. (805175)... Bello Apts. (805115)... Bolts Apts. (805017)... Carlos Apts. (805052)... Los Cuatro Vientos Apts. (805477)... Dallo's Apts. (805284)... Domingo Apts. (805131)... Donath Apts.(2nd) (805120)... Eladio Apts. (805124)... Genaro Apts. (805066)... El Guirre Apts.§ (2nd) (805401)... Humberto Apts. (s/n)... Jornadas Apts. (805047)... Juanita Apts. (805163)... Lola Apts. (805148)... Maribel Apts. (805041)... Medanos Apts. (805480)... La Noria Apts. (805597)... Oasis Apts. (805017/fax 805017)... La Playa Apts.(2nd) (805027)... Rudolfo Apts.§ (805195)... San Jose Apts. (s/n)... Sur Apts. (s/n)... Los Tarajales Apts.§ (2nd) (805301)... Las Tres Palmeras Apts.§ (2nd) (805663/fax805293)... Vistamar Apts. (805525)

VALLE GRAN REY - LA PUNTILLA/CHARCO DEL CONDE APARTMENTS
Baja del Secreto Aparthotel § (805709)... El Bajio Apts. (s/n)... La Casita Apts. (805129)... Charco del Conde Apts.§ (2nd) (805380/fax 805502)... La Condesa Apts.§ (2nd), *La Condesa* (805480)... Sansofe Apts. (805585)

VALLE GRAN REY - VUELTAS APARTMENTS
Abraham Apts. (805424)... Amaya Apts. (800073)... America Apts. (805462)... Avenida Apts. (805461)... Barrera Apts. (805036)... Berta Apts. (805327)... Cabello Apts. (805132)... Casa Pablo Pescador Apts. (805179)... Celia Apts. (805260)... Colon Apts. (805402)... Chijere Darias Apts. (805526)... Chijere Medina Apts. (s/n)... Las Damas Apts. (805052)... Elias & Elias 2 Apts. (805185)... Erasmo Apts.§ (805180)... Francisco Apts. (805649)... Guahedun Apts. (805024)... Humberto Apts. (805451)... Jovel Apts. (805425)... Lilia Apts. (805448)... Manolo Apts. (805260)... Mendoza Apts. (805446)... Miguel 1, 2, 3 Apts.§ (805307)... Montesinos Apts., *Carretera del Puerto* (805048)... Navarro Apts. (805107)... Olivier 1, 2 Apts. (805153)... Omayra Apts. (805667)... Paco Apts. (611361)... Los Pinos Apts. (241679)... La Quema Apts. (805038)... Roni y Lu Apts. (805015)... Sixto Apts. (805332)... Ulises Apts. (805089)... Vidal Apts. (805275)... Vigia del Mar Apts., Lomo Vueltas 6 (805110)... Las Vueltas Apts. (805179)... William Apts. (805646)... Yasmina Apts. (805654)... Yenay Apts. (805471)... Yuremar Apts.§ (2nd) (805360)

VALLE GRAN REY – OTHER APARTMENTS
Casa Policarpo Apts., *El Chorro* (805143)... Flor de Lis Apts., *La Alameda* (805282)...El Mantillo Apts., *El Mantillo* (805053)... Piedra la Garza Apts., *Piedra la Garza* (805332)...

VALLEHERMOSO PENSION
Amaya Pensión*, *Plaza de la Constitución 2*   800073/800077/fax 801138
Pensión Medina Hernandez*, *Plaza de la Constitución* 800023
Pensión Vallehermoso*, *Calle Triana 13*   800283

VALLEHERMOSO APARTMENTS

Amaya Apts, *Plaza de la Constitución* 2   800073/800077/fax 801138
Bernardo Apts., *Calle Triana 4*

Individual houses are available for rent in the following places on Gomera, anticlockwise around the island: San Sebastián, El Cedro, Hermigua (•*Carretera General 265b*, •La Castellana, •El Curato, •Las Hoyetas, •Las Nuevitas, •El Pajarito, •Playa Santa Catalina, •El Tabaibal, •La Vecindad). Agulo, La Palmita, Las Rosas, Vallehermoso (•Los Chapines, •Los Bellos, •El Palmar), Arguamul, Epina, Alojera, Valle Gran Rey (•La Alameda, •El Ancon, •Argaga, •Borbalán, •La Calera, •Cañada La Rosa, •Charco Del Conde, •El Chorro, •La Condesa, •El Entullo, •El Homillo, •Los Hoyitos, •Lomo Riego, •Lomo Vueltas, •El Mantillo, •Las Orijamas, •Las Palmitas, •La Palomera, •Piedra La Garza, •La Pista, •La Playa, •La Puntilla, •Vueltas), Chipude, La Dama, Alajero (ask at the *Columba* bar), Antoncojo, Santiago (•Barranco de Santiago, •Laguna, •Playa, •Tecina), Benchijigua, and El Cabrito.

HERMIGUA SHOPS

Artesania Center, Hermigua   880253

VALLE GRAN REY BOOKSHOPS

El Fotógrafo, La Playa, Valle Gran Rey   805654/fax
Librería Andrés, La Puntilla s/n, Valle Gran Rey   805729/fax 805927

INDEX

Text and maps © copyright Lance Chilton 2000. No part of this publication may be reproduced in any manner without prior permission from the author.

ISBN 1 900802 67 8

COLOURED MAPS OF LA GOMERA AVAILABLE FREE while stocks last: send an A5 self-addressed stamped envelope to
17 Bernard Crescent, Hunstanton PE36 6ER, England.